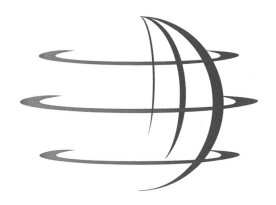

Shipley
Business Development
Lifecycle Guide™

Larry Newman, PPF. APMP

Shipley Associates
532 North 900 West
Kaysville, UT 84037
888.772.WINS (9467)

www.shipleywins.com

First Edition

v1.1.1

First Edition Reprint 2018

ISBN: 978-0-9714244-7-0

This *Business Development Lifecycle Guide* has three aims: 1) Help senior managers design a single, flexible, and scalable business development process based on industry best practices; 2) Help individuals understand the business development process; and 3) Record best practices in a clear, linear order.

Organizations with effective business development processes gain the following benefits:

- Reduced costs and risks of capturing business
- Increased productivity and staff morale
- Improved sales forecasting
- Increased management visibility and control
- More competitive solutions and proposals

The most successful organizations in any market or selling environment innovate and improve framework processes based upon fundamental principles. Less effective organizations follow tightly defined processes, but limited understanding of the fundamental principles reduces their flexibility to adapt to market and customer shifts. The least effective organizations lack consistent processes and fail to understand fundamental principles.

Help senior managers design a single, flexible, and scalable business development process based on industry best practices.

Organizations with a **single** business development process eliminate confusion about which process applies. If you have multiple processes, individuals will repeatedly rationalize why the more disciplined process does not apply to a given opportunity. Business development managers that permit *ad hoc* processes and rely on heroes for success are consistently less successful.

A **flexible** process can be adapted to different types of selling environments, markets, opportunities, and customer requirements.

A **scalable** process can be adapted to differing sizes of opportunities, schedules, resources, and budgets.

As with our *Proposal Guide* and *Capture Guide*, these guidelines are based upon fundamental principles of our consulting practice:

- Align your process to the customer's process.
- Use a disciplined business development process that emphasizes planning.
- Schedule to the process and maintain schedule discipline.

- Base your strategy and tactics on the customer's perspective.
- Maintain customer focus through every step.
- Use DECISION GATE REVIEWS to prompt senior management to decide whether to advance the opportunity to the next phase or end the pursuit.
- Use COLOR TEAM REVIEWS to improve the quality of the business development work product, whether an account plan, pursuit plan, capture plan, strategy, solution, or proposal.

Help individuals understand the business development process.

Whether highly experienced or new to business development, individuals must use common vocabularies and definitions to work effectively and efficiently as a team. Likewise, winning complex, competitive opportunities requires a cohesive, coordinated business development team working with a common understanding of the work process, individual roles, and required tasks.

This *Business Development Lifecycle Guide* is designed to help individuals on your marketing, capture, and proposal teams reach a common understanding of business development process best practices and terms. These fundamental best practices are readily applicable and adaptable when selling to governments and businesses in domestic, international, and export markets; when selling services and products; and in situations requiring security clearances.

Individuals often use common terms with different implicit meanings. Common terms are defined to support cohesive, effective business development teams.

Record best practices in a clear, linear order.

At Shipley Associates, we have observed, studied, and recommended business development best practices since 1972. We endeavor to follow these principles in our consulting practice, teach them in our training practice, apply them in our business development process re-engineering practice, and share them in our series of *Guides*.

This *Business Development Lifecycle Guide* describes a business development process comprising 96 steps divided into seven phases. We urge business development professionals to adapt, scale, and tailor this 96-step process to the types and sizes of business opportunities encountered by their organizations. Managers in organizations pursuing large and small opportunities offering products and services in commercial, export, and government sectors have successfully adapted this process to their unique business environments and circumstances.

All of our *Guides* offer guidelines that reflect best practices but are not meant to be taken as rules. Reality encompasses more shades of gray than can be covered in a guide that is intended to be concise.

This *Business Development Lifecycle Guide* differs from the companion *Proposal Guide* and *Capture Guide*. The *Business Development Lifecycle Guide* is organized linearly from identifying strategic markets to contract award and program initiation. However, the linear treatment is a simplification, as many portions are cyclical within a single pursuit. In addition, business development continues during program execution and service delivery.

In contrast, the *Proposal Guide* and *Capture Guide* are organized alphabetically by topic for rapid, easy reference. A topical reference presumes some understanding of the business development process. Hence, our *Guides* are designed to be used together, so topic sections in the *Proposal Guide* and *Capture Guide* are referenced in this *Business Development Lifecycle Guide*.

Acknowledgements

My thanks go to the many colleagues who collaboratively developed the Shipley 96-Step Business Development Lifecycle Process over more than 25 years. Initial contributors included Terry Bacon, Sid Jensen, David Pugh, and Barbara Von Diether. Subsequent major contributors include Ed Alexander, Tony Birch, Robert Horne, Mike Humm, Nancy Kessler, Walt MacEachern, Howard Nutt, Mark Taylor, David Wagner, and Robert Winslow. Nancy Kessler prepared the initial process step descriptions when managing our Process practice. Brad Douglas urged and supported publication, and Doug Brewer edited initial internal drafts. As the author, I am describing a process that was collaboratively developed and repeatedly improved by multiple Shipley consultants.

Equally important, thank you to my Shipley Partners who supported this work: Frank Howard, Matt King, Howard Nutt, Steve Shipley, and Robert Winslow.

Feedback from our clients and consultants through our consulting practice, business process reengineering practice, and training participants has prompted numerous improvements. Our Shipley licensees and affiliates around the world have also been important contributors and collaborators.

This version for publication was extensively revised to incorporate additional content and cross-referenced to the *Shipley Capture Guide* and *Shipley Proposal Guide*.

About the author

Larry Newman is Vice President and a founding partner of Shipley Associates. He joined Shipley Associates in 1986 as a consultant and training facilitator, helping clients win competitive business in 30 countries and varied selling environments.

Mr. Newman authored all three Shipley Associates *Guides*: *Proposal Guide, Capture Guide,* and *Business Development Lifecycle Guide*. The *Shipley Proposal Guide* was awarded the Society for Technical Communication's Award of Excellence in 2008. With approximately 50,000 copies in print since 1999, the *Shipley Proposal Guide* was selected as the basis for APMP proposal management professional certification. In 2010, he authored the *Shipley Capture Guide*, 2nd Edition. Like the *Proposal Guide*, several organizations have selected it as the basis for professional capture management certification.

He has developed and facilitated numerous Shipley Associates workshops in capture planning, proposal writing and management, executive summary writing, sales writing, and costing. He is an Association of Proposal Management Professionals (APMP) Fellow, is APMP accredited at the Professional level, and has presented at more than 20 professional association conferences. He also developed the *Proposal Guide* podcast series in 2008, downloadable on iTunes.

Derive the greatest benefit from this Business Development Lifecycle Guide in the shortest time by understanding the Shipley business development process and underlying assumptions.

To obtain the greatest benefits from this *Guide*, you should be familiar with:

- Structure of Shipley's 96-step business development process
- Assumptions behind the 96-step business development process
- Organization of this *Guide*
- Suggestions for using this *Guide*

Structure of Shipley's 96-step business development process

The process comprises seven phases, summarized in graphic fashion in figure 1. Phases are separated by decision gate reviews (see figure 2), at which senior management decides whether to advance to the next phase, defer, or end the pursuit. Pursuits that advance through all phases produce new business as contracts are won. Business development comprises a series of these cycles.

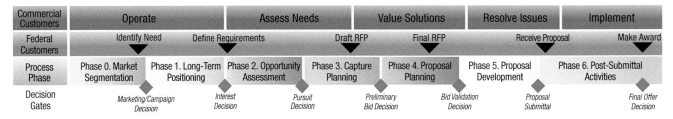

Figure 1. The Business Development Lifecycle. *Phases 0 and 1 link to strategic planning. Phases 2 through 6 align with specific opportunities, and the cycle is repeated for each opportunity. Decision gate reviews delineate the end of one phase and the beginning of the subsequent phase. However, a pursuit might be ended at any decision gate review.*

See DECISION GATE REVIEWS, *Capture Guide.*

While the Shipley 96-Step Process has a long history, it is far from fixed. Up until 1986, it was an 82-step process. The increase from 82 to 96 steps was prompted by our desire to emphasize front-end activity, the development of capture planning as a discipline, and the addition of formal decision gate and color team reviews. We further amended and rebalanced the 96-step process in 1998, when Phase 1 was separated into the 0 and 1 phases, and some of the more detailed proposal preparation steps were consolidated.

PRECIPITATING CUSTOMER ACTION	PHASE	DECISION GATE	OBJECTIVE
	0	Marketing/ Campaign	Verify market/customer fits your strategic focus.
Begin assessing needs and developing acquisition plan.	1	Interest	Verify the opportunity fits your strategic direction and capability.
Begin developing requirements.	2	Pursuit	Verify opportunity warrants forming capture team and funding capture actions.
Begin refining requirements; release draft bid request.	3	Preliminary Bid	Verify you are positioned to win before committing to an expensive proposal effort.
Release final bid request, contract expiring, accept white paper or study recommendations.	4	Bid Validation	Verify "show stoppers" have been addressed.
Proposals are due.	5	Proposal Submittal	Verify proposal is compliant, responsive, competitive, and conforms to organizational standards.
Contract offered to winner.	6	Final Offer	Verify contract offers acceptable risks and rewards.

Figure 2. Decision Gate Review Objectives. *Decision gate review decisions should be made no later than the event listed in "Precipitating Customer Action." The ultimate objectives of this phased approach are to allocate sufficient resources to the most "winnable" opportunities. Note that Phase 0 and 1 gate reviews are not opportunity specific, and the Phase 6 gate is simultaneously the last gate in business development and the first gate in program execution.*

Assumptions behind the 96-step business development process

The Shipley 96-step process incorporates the following assumptions:

- Each phase is delineated by decision gate reviews. If you have not passed a decision gate review, you are in the same phase, independent of the customer's activities. You have simply not reacted to the customer's and competitors' actions.

- A single process eliminates "shopping" for the most convenient process for each opportunity. The 96-step process is only a starting point. Tailor it to your organization and selling environment.

- While the process appears to be linear, it is cyclical within phases and overall. Many times, the specific order of tasks within a phase is unimportant. Indeed, some tasks routinely belong in different phases within certain markets or organizations, reinforcing the need to tailor the process.

- Flexibility and scalability are incorporated by merging or splitting phases, and then by adding or deleting steps within phases.

See PROCESS, *Capture Guide.*

Organization of this *Guide*

This Process *Guide* is organized to match the 96-step business development lifecycle chart, included as an insert with this *Guide*. The chart is inserted so you can view the chart while turning and reading pages. Figure 3 shows the chart in thumbnail form and is not intended to be readable as shown.

Consider the structure of the 96-step process chart. The seven business development phases, depicted in different colors, are separated into discrete tasks or steps, shown in different colors. Role identifiers on the left side of the chart show which roles support each task (shown by where the horizontal lines extending from the role identifiers intersect task boxes). Four distinct colored bars on the top of the chart approximate how tasks align with customer activities:

- *Commercial Customers* indicates customers' generic focus as they advance through their buying cycle, and it applies broadly to all potential customers. *Operate* is the ongoing steady state until some internal or external event prompts a customer to assess whether they might benefit by changing their current approach. *Assess Needs* is where latent needs become explicit. Here, value-added sellers collaboratively help customers define requirements. *Value Solutions* is where customers assess the relative value of different solutions to their organization and to themselves personally. *Resolve Issues* is where customers tentatively select a solution and source, and then revisit the risk of that solution and source. *Implement* is where customers implement the solution, and sellers reinforce the value delivered and position subsequent sales. In general, this marks the presumed end of a cyclical process and return to the *Operate* or even *Assess Needs* phases.

- *Federal Customers* is approximately aligned with the U.S. federal government acquisition process, but many aspects are similar to buying processes of other national, state, and regional government entities.

- *Process Phase* lists the seven phases. Note that decision gate reviews delineate phases and should be conducted proactively before or promptly after the precipitating customer event.

- *Milestones* lists decision gates, key milestones, team reviews, and major events.

The *Sample Time Frame* bar across the bottom shows a representative timeline for each phase. The times listed are approximate and often related to customer events. In general, if the overall procurement process shortens, the phases also shorten. However, the timing of steps within a phase is largely governed by management's assessment of available resources and the thoroughness and efficiency of their business development processes.

The *Documents and Results* items displayed across the bottom are commonly produced within the phase and are associated with the steps shown. Documents are critically important for three reasons:

- The document is often the only tangible evidence that a task has been completed.

- The quality of the document is often the only means to assess the quality of the work.

- Document content can be shared among the team and with teammates.

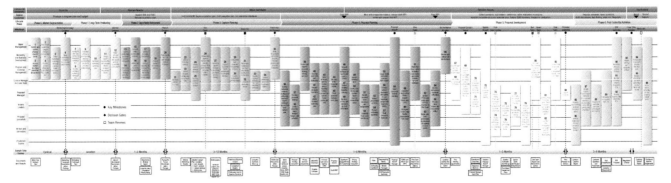

Figure 3. The Shipley 96-Step Business Development Process. *The 7 phases and 96 steps are an efficient basis to understand and develop a framework process for your organization. The full-scale, fold-out, 96-step process chart is an unbound insert designed to be viewable while referring to this Business Development Lifecycle Guide.*

For example, an individual might claim to have designed a winning solution, but until it can be communicated to the rest of the business development team, persuasively presented to the customer, accurately costed, competitively priced, and eventually delivered, it has minimal value to the seller or customer.

Within this *Business Development Lifecycle Guide*, each phase is briefly described in order, and relevant steps are shown graphically as a subset of the 96-step chart. Following each phase description, encompassed steps are described in order with cross-references to relevant *Capture Guide* and *Proposal Guide* topic sections.

Business development roles and responsibilities are summarized in Appendix A. Regard these descriptions as a starting point, as titles, roles, and responsibilities vary widely. Many industry colleagues will also share role descriptions used in their organizations if asked. Shipley's 96-step business development process and framework are available by subscription as an interactive, web-based tool. Use it to access descriptions of each phase and step in the lifecycle, integrated with topic sections of the *Shipley Capture Guide* and *Proposal Guide*.

Access the online business development chart via this link:

http://sbdl.shipleywins.com

Acronyms used in this *Guide* are defined in Appendix B. Acronyms are coined, changed, and eliminated frequently, so the full range of acronyms likely to be encountered in various selling environments and markets could not possibly be included. For more help, consult current, readily accessible web sources as needed.

Suggestions for using the process

Here are some suggestions on using the 96-step business development process:

- Review every step using the process chart like a checklist to prompt you to consider if that step is necessary.

- Eliminate unnecessary or irrelevant steps. For example, if teaming is not involved, eliminate steps involving teaming.

- Tailor the entire process to each environment and situation. For example, in an Indefinite Delivery Indefinite Quantity (IDIQ) or a task order environment with a 10-day proposal response, many steps and reviews must be eliminated. When selling services, the manufacturing-oriented steps would be eliminated but management processes increasingly emphasized. Similarly, add selected steps for export and secure bids.

- Consider if needed or customary steps should be added because of characteristics of your organization or market.

- Avoid eliminating steps because you lack the resources to complete them. Management needs to know if resources are unavailable. Decide whether they want to assume the risk and understand the importance of those potentially overlooked steps. Reassess the impact of eliminating steps when documenting lessons learned.

- Post the 96-step process chart or your tailored replacement prominently in view of your capture and proposal development teams. Repeatedly note where you are in the process to emphasize the importance of early steps.

- When prompted by a customer event or assigned a task by your management, look upstream and downstream. Look upstream to assess what has been done, what should have been done, and which steps you must still complete. Then look downstream to identify and schedule what remains to be done as you develop your own work plan and schedule. For example, if a bid request is released, your management decides to bid, and you are assigned as the proposal manager, assess prior steps. Which steps were missed but essential? Which subsequent steps are essential? Then schedule these tasks. Assign a single task owner for each step, and manage your plan with primary focus on your next scheduled decision gate review, color team review, or major event.

Table of Contents

Preface . . . . *iii*
Using the Shipley Business Development Lifecycle Guide . . . . *vi*

Phase 0: Market Segmentation

1 Identify and explore strategic market areas. 2
2 Assess market direction, potentials, and postures 2
3 Benchmark capabilities, analyze strategic relationships, etc. 2
4 Position assets (alliances, acquisitions, R&D, capital, etc.). 3
5 Define marketing/campaign strategy options; make recommendations. 3
6 Make marketing/campaign decision and deploy teams 4

Phase 1: Long-Term Positioning

7 Investigate data and options in marketing/campaign area 6
8 Develop and align marketing/campaign plan. 6
9 Establish criteria to prioritize new business opportunities and build prospect relationships 6
10 Implement marketing/campaign plan 8
11 Target specific opportunities and prepare interest decision recommendation 8
12 Make interest decision and assign lead for opportunity assessment 9

Phase 2: Opportunity Assessment

13 Gather preliminary customer/program intelligence 11
14 Participate in industry briefings and other meetings. 11
15 Cultivate initial position with customer. 11
16 Understand basic customer requirements. 11
17 Define probable competitors 12
18 Analyze business fit, competitive potential, and initial competitive pricing range. 12
19 Prepare pursuit recommendations 13
20 Make pursuit decision and assign capture manager 13

Phase 3: Capture Planning

21 Establish capture core team 15
22 Extend customer contacts. 16
23 Gather program intelligence and analyze data 16
24 Initiate capture strategy and plan 17
25 Develop capture/proposal budget 18
26 Review and approve capture plan and win strategy (Blue Team review); schedule status reviews 19
27 Implement capture strategy, action plans, and initial pricing strategy 19
28 Support customer needs analysis and requirements definition. 19
29 Collaborate with customer on potential solution 20
30 Update competitive pricing range 20
31 Make early make/buy decision and initiate teaming/subcontractors 21
32 Conduct Black Hat review. 22
33 Update capture strategy; mock up executive summary 22
34 Prepare preliminary bid/no-bid recommendations. 23
35 Make preliminary bid/no-bid decision; dedicate program and proposal managers 25

Phase 4: Proposal Planning

36 Extend customer contacts, intelligence gathering, and tech/mgmt/cost/price approaches from capture plan 27

37 Develop proposal strategy 27

38 Define proposal tasks, detailed budget, and schedule 28

39 Review and approve proposal strategy, pricing, and cost 30

40 Develop draft WBS and dictionary 30

41 Prepare program schedule 31

42 Initiate detailed make/buy plan 31

43 Write in-house, subcontractor, and/or teaming SOW(s); account for subcontractor pricing and cost 31

44 Develop initial proposal outline 32

45 Draft proposal management plan. 33

46 Support customer definition of needs and requirements 33

47 Define detailed baseline offering. 33

48 Receive, review, and comment on draft solicitation 34

49 Update winning price. 37

50 Define cost drivers and update target price in competitive range. 35

51 Identify proposal team members and assignments. 36

52 Establish team area and library 36

53 Initiate preparation of PDWs. 37

54 Prepare estimating guidelines. 37

55 Create a SOW/WBS/BOE responsibility matrix 38

56 Prepare writers' packages and gather re-use materials; assign cost bogies to BOEs 38

57 Draft executive summary 38

58 Hold proposal kickoff meeting 39

59 Complete and review PDWs; prepare mockups/OPPs 40

60 Hold peer review and finalize materials for Pink Team 40

61 Hold Pink Team review, including cost volume and initial bottom-up cost estimate. 41

62 Update PDWs and mockups/OPPs in response to Pink Team 42

63 Begin early draft/presentation development (if required to meet goals). 42

64 Receive and analyze customer solicitation 42

65 Prepare final bid/no-bid recommendation 43

66 Review and validate the bid decision 43

Phase 5: Proposal Development

67 Finalize team and subcontractor relationships 45

68 Attend the pre-proposal conference. 45

69 Impose solution freeze; finalize WBS and WBS dictionary, SOW(s), responsibility matrix, program schedule,
    make/buy plan, etc. 46

70 Create compliance checklists, proposal response matrix, etc.. 47

71 Finalize proposal management plan. 48

72 Hold proposal update kickoff meeting 49

73 Finalize/review PDWs and mockups/OPPs in response to customer solicitation 49

74 Develop proposal text/visuals or script/presentation/video. 50

75 Write task description estimates and rationales. 50

76 Roll up and review costing figures 51

77 Hold status and compliance review meetings. 51

78 Review drafts and visuals; rehearse presentation. 51

79 Prepare proposal drafts/presentation and costs for Red Team, and if separate, Green Team reviews 52

80 Hold Red Team review, including price, or separate Red and Green Team reviews. 53

81 Address Red Team and Green Team comments and finalize draft/presentation/video 54

82 Conduct final compliance check and "publish" proposal deliverables 55

83 Conduct final legal, cost, and management reviews; hold Gold Team. 55

84 Submit proposal 55

Phase 6: Post-Submittal Activities

85 Organize and maintain proposal documentation 57

86 Identify, write, and transmit proposal lessons learned. 57

87 Update capture plan/closure strategies for customer questions, discussions, orals, FPR pricing, and negotiation. . . . 58

88 Respond to customer questions and support fact finding. 59

89 Participate in discussions, orals, etc. 59

90 Revalidate proposal pricing strategy 65

91 Receive customer request; respond to FPR 60

92 Review, approve, and submit the FPR 60

93 Update strategy and negotiate contract 60

94 Prepare and implement program transition plan 61

95 Request and attend customer debriefing; conduct White Hat review. 62

96 Hold a victory party (win or lose), including review teams 62

Appendix A: Roles and Responsibilities

Capture Manager 63

Program Manager. 64

Orals Coach. 64

Volume Manager/Leader. 65

Technical/Proposal Writer 65

Desktop Publisher 66

Graphic Specialist 66

Proposal Editor 67

Proposal Coordinator 67

Contract Administrator 68

Cost Volume Manager. 68

IMP/IMS Specialist. 69

Price-to-Win Specialist 69

Program Manager. 70

Appendix B: Acronyms *71*

Appendix C: Interactive Shipley Business Development Lifecycle™ Tool *72*

Index *73*

Market Segmentation is the process of defining and sub-dividing a large market into segments that exhibit similar needs, wants, or demand characteristics. Your objective is to develop a marketing mix that aligns with your customers' expectations by market segment, geography, and culture. Few organizations are big enough or equipped to competitively meet the demands of all segments, so you must chose the segments that you are best equipped to satisfy.

The steps shown in figure 4 evaluate your marketplace and identify segments of the market in which you want to compete.

To successfully develop new, long-term revenue streams, select business segments that align with your corporate strategic plan. Identify and focus your marketing efforts on selected segments before you target discrete opportunities.

Business developers who target specific opportunities before they understand a market segment win fewer opportunities at greater expense, and they introduce additional risk.

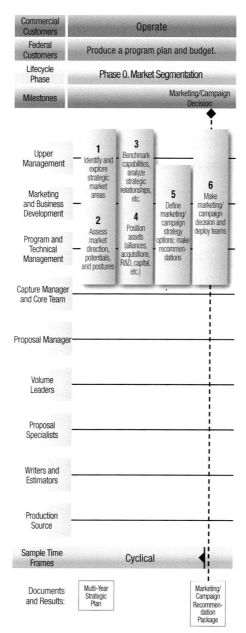

Figure 4. Phase 0: Market Segmentation. *This phase includes tasks to characterize markets and decide the types of business you will pursue. Make a marketing/campaign decision before targeting specific opportunities. Phase 0 begins with the identification and exploration of strategic market areas and ends with the decision to pursue a strategic market area.*

1 Identify and explore strategic market areas

1

Identify and explore strategic market areas

Stemming from your strategic plan, identify, define, and explore market segments that align with your strategic plan.

Consider the behavioral, demographic, geographic, regulatory, and psychographic characteristics of customers by segment. Note that psychographic characteristics refer to the desired benefits sought by customers in that market segment.

Decide how you are going to meet customers' demands. This may include Research and Development (R&D) investments, reorganization, new business acquisition, divestitures, joint ventures, or teaming arrangements.

Documents and Results

- Multi-year strategic plan

2 Assess market direction, potentials, and postures

2

Assess market direction, potentials, and postures

Once desired customers/new market areas are identified in Step 1, examine each potential target area to gather as much information as possible. Analysis transforms information into intelligence.

Gather and analyze additional information on:

- Customer wants, needs, and problems
- Customer satisfaction with past or current contracts
- Customer budgets, schedules, and plans
- State-of-the-art technology and trends
- Business trends and practices
- Procurement policies and practices
- Competitors' technical capability, quality, cost competitiveness, and production methods

Using this intelligence, determine which market segments you will pursue and how you will pursue them. Focus resources on obtainable target markets, avoid wasting resources on opportunities beyond corporate competencies or capabilities, or diluting your focus by targeting too many market segments.

For each market segment, determine the competitors and their positions with the customers. Is the market expanding, static, mature, or emerging? Can you win additional new market share, or will you have to take business away from a current provider? What is the potential profit from these new markets?

3 Benchmark capabilities, analyze strategic relationships, etc.

3

Benchmark capabilities, analyze strategic relationships, etc.

Benchmark your offerings from customers' perspectives, considering their visions, objectives, hot button issues, and requirements.

Assess your capabilities, assets, and risks against the competition and market leaders. What are your relative strengths and weaknesses? Do you have or can you acquire the assets required to compete? What are the risks of new offerings and the potential impact on existing offerings?

How do you rate against best practice? Evaluate how your capabilities align with potential customers' short- and long-term needs and requirements.

What strategic partnerships are in place or needed to establish credibility in the market? Is there a current or potential strategic partner who is well-positioned in the market segment? How can each alliance be leveraged? Are customers in that market segment prone to select teams, which include certain types of organizations (e.g., small and small disadvantaged businesses) or favor pre-qualified suppliers? If such a strategic relationship does not exist, how can one be formed that would support your entry?

4

4
Position assets (alliances, acquisitions, R&D, capital, etc.)

Position assets (alliances, acquisitions, R&D, capital, etc.)

Management develops or acquires and then positions the resources to meet corporate objectives. You must be organized and have subsystems and procedures in place to support sound market decisions. This includes:

- Developing marketing capability to position your organization
- Developing adequate systems to gather, analyze, and exploit marketing intelligence
- Orchestrating intelligence-gathering systems to provide marketplace, customer, and competitive information
- Providing technical expertise to analyze barriers to entry and identify gaps in your current capabilities
- Identifying and staffing R&D requirements
- Participating in professional societies to gain exposure and capture competitive and technical intelligence
- Organizing and aligning sales and BD resources to the market

- Attending trade shows to promote your organization and capabilities while gathering market information
- Preparing and presenting technical papers
- Identifying capability or resource gaps

Marketing, business development, and *sales* are terms with different meanings in different organizations and environments. In the broadest sense, marketing and business development are synonyms. However, in the context of this *Guide*, business development is roughly divided into marketing and sales. Marketing comprises the activities that position an organization in their target market segments. Sales comprises the activities focused on winning specific orders. A campaign comprises a set of marketing activities designed to position an organization to sell their services or products to a specific, targeted market segment.

5

5
Define marketing/ campaign strategy options; make recommen- dations

Define marketing/campaign strategy options; make recommendations

Based on the outcomes of Steps 1–4, management defines specific market segment objectives. These objectives might include exploiting existing strengths, moving into other new strategic markets, developing new products or services, or abandoning markets that provide little potential. Your near-term strategic marketing plan might position your organization for long-term work.

Consider the following factors when assessing marketing/campaign strategy options:

- Fit to strategic business plan
- Market match or expansion
- Product/service match or expansion
- Risk
- Cost of pursuing the market
- Financial return
- Positioning for future business
- Competition

To enhance your position in a particular market segment, link each factor to specific strategies and implementation tactics. Prepare to brief senior management as part of the Marketing/ Campaign Decision Gate review.

Identify and seek management's approval and commitment of resources for R&D, divestitures, mergers, acquisitions and joint ventures, or reorganizations, as needed to pursue these market segments. At regular intervals, review and update market segment campaign plans.

The marketing plan must address the target markets' competitive landscape, financial objectives and budgets risks, and your ability to outperform competitors. External resources are often necessary to collect and analyze competitive data, including the past performance of potential competitors.

6 Make marketing/campaign decision and deploy teams

If senior management decides to proceed, the marketing teams begin to gather additional relevant information on each approved market segment and to identify potential opportunity clusters and prospects in each segment.

The marketing team consists of representatives from:

- Senior management
- Sales, marketing, and BD
- Program and technical management

As additional information is gathered and assessed, the overall campaign assumptions and recommendations must be reevaluated and confirmed, modified, or dropped. The timing for subsequent reviews should be specified by senior management as an output of a positive Marketing/Campaign Decision Gate review.

Depending upon the organization and selling environment, many business development executives will ask their account managers, marketers, or field sales professionals to prepare account plans. Account plans tend to be more complete in market segments where customers and sellers have ongoing relationships. In entirely new market segments, account plans might not be prepared until after an Interest Decision Gate review. Organizations that focus primarily on large government opportunities often forego account plans and focus solely on preparing capture plans for specific, defined opportunities.

Milestones

- Marketing/campaign decision

Documents and Results

- Marketing/campaign recommendation package
- Account Plans (optional)

Long-Term Positioning encompasses activities that establish your place in the market, influence potential customers' perceptions, and prospect for business opportunities, which might fit with your strategic plans and capabilities.

Unfortunately, sole source awards of significance are rare. The next best option is to position your organization and eventual solution as the customer's preferred option.

Steps 7–12 (see figure 5) must be done early and repeated on a cyclical basis, long before focusing on specific opportunities in your chosen market segments, to build name recognition, showcase your capabilities, and build credible relationships with customers and potential teaming partners.

See DECISION GATE REVIEWS, *Capture Guide.*

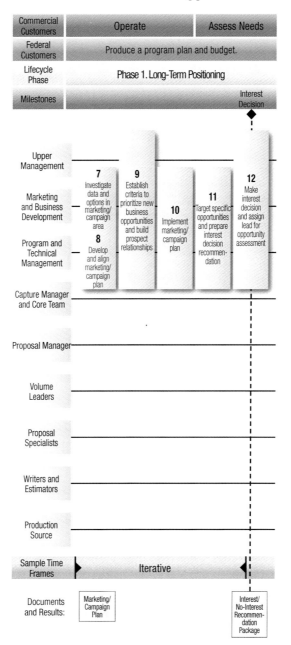

Figure 5. Phase 1: Long-Term Positioning. *This phase encompasses your efforts to generate or discover opportunities you might decide to pursue and bid. It culminates with an Interest Decision Gate review. Often, the interest decision is delegated to business development staff who routinely evaluate opportunities for matches with organization capabilities. The interest decision simply means the opportunity looks promising enough to justify background research and initial contacts with the customer.*

7 — Investigate data and options in marketing/campaign area

7

Investigate data and options in marketing/campaign area

See DECISION GATE REVIEWS, *Capture Guide.*

Data are just data; they need interpretation or analysis to make them relevant. Data must be current. Review data developed in Steps 2–4 leading to the Marketing/Campaign Decision gate review, and determine if these data are still current. Re-analyze and reinterpret changed and new data. Identify and account for any data dependencies and note the impact on your strategic options.

Based upon Marketing/Campaign Decision Gate review directives at the end of Phase 0, define the strategies and tactics to achieve the desired position in this market segment.

Identify cost, sales, and technology strategies that will drive you to your desired position. Quantify the cost to revisit your market and customer analysis, enhance your competitive analysis, and implement your positioning strategies and tactics.

Are there other untapped sources of information or market research not previously available? Are more market studies needed? Do you need outside, third-party advice? Are your data complete? Can you build necessary customer relationships in the time required?

8 — Develop and align marketing/campaign plan

8

Develop and align marketing/campaign plan

See CAPTURE PLANNING and STRATEGY, *Capture Guide.*

Using the outputs of Step 7, develop a marketing/campaign plan package. Typical components include:

- Ultimate customer profile: vision, hot button issues, and requirements
- Market drivers
- Opportunity sector profiles
- Analysis of strengths and weaknesses of potential competitors
- Assessment of market posture
- Market area strategies

- Resource requirements and deployment plan
- Market area performance goals and return-on-investment analysis

Adjust the plan to reflect decision makers' directives from the Marketing/Campaign Decision Gate review, incorporate new intelligence, and realign the plan with your strategic plan.

Documents and Results

- Marketing/campaign plan

9 — Establish criteria to prioritize new business opportunities and build prospect relationships

9

Establish criteria to prioritize new business opportunities and build prospect relationships

See INTRODUCTION TO CAPTURE PLANNING, *Capture Guide.*

Define criteria to prioritize the new business opportunities required to reach strategic goals and objectives (see figure 6). Consider these factors:

- Potential for additional business
- Product, market, and technology match
- Return on investment
- Fit to strategic business plan objectives
- Corporate risks
- Knowledge of the marketplace and competition

- Projected long-term business conditions
- Competitive environment
- Chances of being successful
- Market costs
- Costs of winning business
- Resource commitment for the capture effort as well as program execution

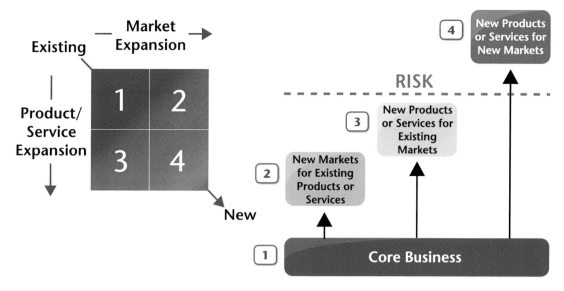

Figure 6. **Avenues to Increase Revenue.** *To meet revenue growth goals, most organizations must expand beyond core business areas, as shown on the right. Sector 2, the least risky expansion, is to offer proven products or services to new markets because you can predictably price and deliver. Sector 3, offering new products and services to existing markets and familiar customers, might seem less risky, but a stumble threatens current revenue. Recent research suggests selling new services or products to existing markets might be easier, and the relative risk varies. Sector 4, taking new products and services to new markets, requires solid strategic, business, and market planning and is beyond the normal scope of capture planning. The graphic on the right illustrates the increasing risk associated with market, service, and product expansions. The numbers align with the numbered sectors listed in figure 7.*

New business opportunities that are classified as *strategic* or *must win* attract more attention within an organization to the detriment of routine opportunities. Given the four opportunity sectors shown in figure 7, sector 1 opportunities are usually the most winnable and least risky.

In Sectors 2–4, a new customer relationship must be built. Even with existing customers, the introduction of a new offering demands a redefined relationship. The business development team must establish or modify these relationships while implementing new positioning strategies.

See DECISION GATE REVIEWS, Capture Guide.

SECTOR	CHARACTERISTICS	PURSUIT INDICATION	EARLY ACTION
1	Similar product or service, similar market	Strong	Focus on competitors
2	Same product or service, new customers	Moderate	Learn market, establish presence
3	Similar customers, new product or service	Moderate	Verify needs of customers
4	New product or service, new customers	Weak	Create detailed plan, commit resources, revisit your strategic plan

Figure 7. **Choosing Opportunities.** *Be realistic when branching out from your core business. Opportunities in Sector 1 of the chart above automatically carry a strong pursuit indication. Actions and decisions will often be focused on competitors. Sector 2 opportunities should be weighed against your emerging view of the new market and the success you have had establishing your presence. Sector 3 lead considerations should concentrate on verifying needs of the unfamiliar customer. Sector 4 ventures demand detailed planning, inevitably consume more resources before a new customer can be influenced to purchase something you have little history selling, and often warrant revisiting your strategic plan.*

10 Implement marketing/campaign plan

10
Implement marketing/ campaign plan

See PERSUASION, PRESENTATIONS TO CUSTOMERS, SALES LETTERS, CUSTOMER-FOCUSED CAPTURE SKILLS AND TACTICS, MODEL DOCUMENT 1, *and* TAILORING A CAPTURE TEMPLATE-ACTION PLANS, *Capture Guide.*

Assign actions from Step 8 to specific individuals with deadlines and follow-up actions.

Marketing initiates activities designed to position your organization to win business in the prioritized list of opportunities. These activities often include:

- White papers
- Advertising
- Direct mail
- Trade shows
- Speeches
- Articles in professional journals
- Upper management visits
- R&D programs
- Website focus
- Technical visits

The most effective way to influence customers to prefer your organization and solution is through quality performance on ongoing work and by collaborating with them on potential work. Your "call plan" or "customer contact plan" should identify:

- Person to be contacted (name, title, contact information)
- Objective of the call
- Relationship to potential opportunities
- Customer "hot buttons"
- Person from your organization making the contact
- Deadline to make the contact and report on the results

Building customer relationships and establishing trust are key activities during these early phases of the BD lifecycle.

11 Target specific opportunities and prepare interest decision recommendation

11
Target specific opportunities and prepare interest decision recommen-dation

See DECISION GATE REVIEWS, *Capture Guide.*

Within the framework described in Steps 9 and 10, identify specific potential opportunities, projects, programs, or purchases. For each one, identify the purchase cycle, decision makers, budget, and other opportunity-specific information.

Discard opportunities with low win probability or poor strategic potential so time and money can be focused on more promising targets (see figure 8).

The interest decision might be the most important decision gate in business development. Once approved, an interest decision acquires momentum and is increasingly difficult to terminate at subsequent pursuit and bid decision gates. Reviewers in many organizations lack the will to say "No" and lament prior approvals. "No" must be acceptable. "Yes" implies an alternative opportunity is not pursued.

If opportunities meet the qualification criteria established in step 9, prepare to present your analysis and recommendations to senior management at the Interest Decision Gate review. Mandatory and optional inputs for this review should be predefined and aligned with your qualification criteria. Typically, larger, must-win opportunities will have more rigorous briefing input requirements.

Figure 8. The Opportunity Funnel. *The goal of a rational BD process is to eliminate opportunities with poor strategic potential or low win probability. Organizations that eliminate poor opportunities early in the process actually increase total revenues. Win the most important contracts by concentrating your resources.*

12

12

Make interest decision and assign lead for opportunity assessment

See DECISION GATE REVIEWS, *Capture Guide;* APPENDIX A: ROLES AND RESPONSIBILITIES.

Make interest decision and assign lead for opportunity assessment

The objective of the Interest Decision Gate review is to verify that the opportunity fits your organization's strategic direction and capability. If approved, management authorizes additional research to assess the opportunity, or opportunities, and the activities to position your organization and potential solutions.

If the interest decision is positive, management assigns a lead individual to complete or manage the in-depth opportunity assessment.

The title of this lead individual might be account manager, sales director, marketing specialist, territory manager, or another title, depending upon the organization, but he or she is not yet the capture manager.

Milestones

- Interest decision

Documents and Results

- Interest/no-interest recommendation package

Opportunity Assessment builds knowledge of the opportunity, the customer, and the competitive circumstances to support a decision on whether to begin active pursuit.

Focus Opportunity Assessment business development activities (see figure 9) focus on the following tasks:

- Identify and confirm data from the account plan, if used, to prepare an opportunity analysis report as input for the Pursuit Decision Gate review.

- Establish the initial competitive pricing range, sometimes called the price to compete.

- Analyze the customer, competitors, and your organization relative to a specific opportunity or set of opportunities.

- Estimate the resource and investment requirements needed to win, with emphasis on the upcoming capture planning phase.

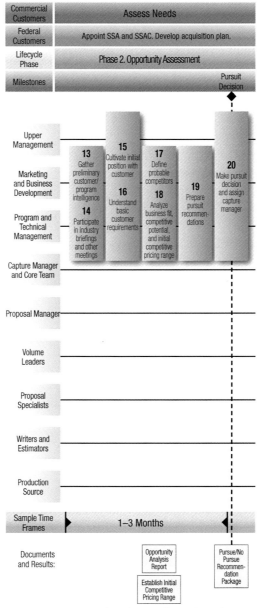

Figure 9. Phase 2: Opportunity Assessment. *This phase is focused on the customer, potential competitors, and the opportunity. It includes basic research to determine whether the organization should commit further resources to develop a capture plan and influence the customer to prefer your solution. A positive pursuit decision confirms that the opportunity matches corporate strategic directions, fits within core competencies, and that the customer might be influenced to prefer, or at least seriously consider, an offer your organization could make. An affirmative pursuit decision launches the capture planning phase.*

13 Gather preliminary customer/program intelligence

13
Gather preliminary customer/ program intelligence

See Customer-Focused Capture Skills and Tactics, *and* Presentations to Customers, *Capture Guide.*

Begin to work with the customer by positioning yourself as capable of understanding the customer's needs, helping them define requirements, and potentially providing an acceptable or preferred solution.

Successful intelligence gathering requires that you:

- Listen to the customer
- Ask good questions

- Determine customer issues
- Provide feedback to demonstrate that you understand the customer's needs
- Identify the decision maker, potential budget, funding source, buying and evaluation process, funding status, and customer's view of you and your competition

14 Participate in industry briefings and other meetings

14
Participate in industry briefings and other meetings

Participation in industry briefings and meetings is essential to demonstrate interest and is often mandatory to be able to submit a bid. Carefully target these intelligence gathering and positioning opportunities, select appropriate people to attend, and then strategize your approach to each event.

In this step, the marketing team characterizes the attractiveness of individual opportunities for pursuit. Exploit industry days, pre-bidders conferences, and similar events as a valuable forum to build customer relationships, network with potential teaming partners, and gather competitive intelligence.

15 Cultivate initial position with customer

15
Cultivate initial position with customer

Upper management, marketing, and technical personnel cultivate customer relationships by collaborating with them during visits, giving presentations on technology and capabilities, issuing white papers, and inviting customer decision makers for plant visits and demonstrations.

Build a relationship with your target customers. Repeated, positive, and predictable contact with customers helps you build a trusting relationship and foster further access to key decision makers and influencers.

16 Understand basic customer requirements

16
Understand basic customer requirements

See Value Propositions, *Proposal Guide.*

Validate your understanding of the customer's needs and requirements. This may require going deeper than just requirements; discover what drives the requirements, what interface needs might exist, and what may motivate the customer to buy. Identify the technical requirements, management requirements, deliverables, preferred schedule, awardable budget, and the type and sources of funds.

Make sure there is a business case to advance the opportunity. Consider the business case for both the customer and your organization. Begin to develop and quantify the value proposition for both organizations. While you might pursue an initially unprofitable opportunity due to the longer-term profit potential, most opportunities must be profitable individually to secure management capture planning funding.

17 Define probable competitors

17
Define probable competitors

Develop a list of probable competitors based upon market history and discussions with marketing personnel, program management, sales, and other personnel who know the customer and competitors. Repeatedly refine this list based on new discussions with the customer, key suppliers, subcontractors, and other sources of competitive intelligence.

If this is a re-compete, consider making a Freedom of Information Act (FOIA) request of the winning proposal and contract for the previous two competitions. Even if you are the incumbent, determine who might seek to regain their prior contract. FOIA requests might take up to 6 months to obtain, so start early.

18 Analyze business fit, competitive potential, and initial competitive pricing range

18
Analyze business fit, competitive potential, and initial competitive pricing range

Review what has been learned about the customer, market segment, and competitors. Decide if you are adequately capitalized and staffed to pursue, capture, win, and execute an opportunity (see figure 10). Decide if the opportunity aligns with corporate strategic goals. Even if moving into a new market or creating a new customer is in the strategic plan, does it make sense? Can you afford to lose? Can you afford to win?

Build and repeatedly update your competitor, competitive, and price-to-win analysis knowledge base from publicly available, legally and ethically obtainable open-source information. If you are uncomfortable with the source, do not use it.

Documents and Results

- Opportunity analysis report
- Establish initial competitive pricing range

See DECISION GATE REVIEWS, PRICING TO WIN, PROCESS, *Capture Guide;* and BID DECISIONS, *Proposal Guide.*

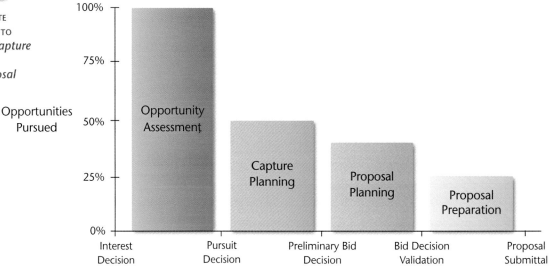

Figure 10. Selecting Good Opportunities. *After the initial affirmative opportunity assessment, repeatedly reassess whether to continue to pursue each opportunity at successive decision gate reviews. Unaccepting customers, superior competitors, insufficient budgets, and poorly written proposals are valid reasons to cease pursuit. The notional percentage of opportunities allowed through each decision gate depends on characteristics of the market, company objectives, and quality of business leads. The most successful organizations often submit proposals on 25 percent or fewer of the opportunities identified. Establish criteria for each decision gate review in advance, or discipline will fail and resources will be wasted.*

19

19
Prepare pursuit recommen- dations

Prepare pursuit recommendations

As stated earlier, the focus of business development activities in the Opportunity Assessment phase were threefold:

- Migrate data from the account plan, if used, to draft initial portions of the capture plan and capture strategy.
- Analyze the customer, competitors, and yourselves relative to the specific opportunity or set of opportunities.
- Estimate the resource and investment requirements needed to win, with emphasis on the upcoming capture planning phase.

Base your recommendation on the business fit, competitive analysis, priority of other business opportunities, and availability of resources.

Provide unbiased, objective information. Do not over- or under-sell an opportunity. Consider profit potential, pursuit resources, win probability, positioning for future work, and opportunity cost of not pursuing other opportunities.

20

20
Make pursuit decision and assign capture manager

See DECISION GATE REVIEWS, *Capture Guide.*

Make pursuit decision and assign capture manager

Answer these questions at the Pursuit Decision Gate review:

- Does the opportunity meet the strategic business plan?
- Are we known to the customer?
- Does the customer rely on us for input and assistance?
- Does the customer have a budget and, if so, what is it?
- Is the opportunity real? Is there proof?
- Can we deliver what the customer wants, in all aspects?
- Are we, or is anyone else, favored by the customer?
- What resources or costs are required to pursue this lead?
- How does this opportunity affect our current business?
- What are the risks of bidding? of losing? of winning? of performing?
- What is our expected return on investment?

Except for a do-not-pursue decision, the primary output of the Pursuit Decision Gate review is to name the capture manager and initiate the development of the capture plan. While the individual who first identified the opportunity is often placed in the capture manager role, this is not always the best choice. Perhaps the marketer or account manager cannot be spared from continuing marketing or sales activities.

The capture manager directs the capture triumvirate, including the program manager and proposal manager, further distancing them from their full-time job of selling and developing business. In addition, the capture manager role is often not a full-time position, but the time requirements tend to increase as the opportunity progresses.

Milestones

- Pursuit decision

Documents and Results

- Pursue/no pursue recommendation package

Capture Planning focuses on preparing and reviewing the capture plan and then implementing strategies to influence the customer to prefer your solution. Capture planning continues until the pursuit is terminated, or the contract is won.

The primary outputs of the Pursuit Decision Gate review in Phase 2 were the decision to pursue and the naming of a capture manager. While Phase 2 Opportunity Assessment activities include early capture planning activities, a capture team is formed and a capture plan drafted, reviewed, and

implemented in Phase 3 Capture Planning (see figure 11). Color team reviews within Phase 3 are designed to improve the quality of the capture planning effort. The customer's decision to seek a proposal is the usual event that signals the end of this phase and the initiation of Phase 4 Proposal Planning.

See CAPTURE PLANNING, COLOR TEAM REVIEWS, GATE DECISION REVIEWS, PRICING TO WIN, *and* VALUE PROPOSITION, *Capture Guide*.

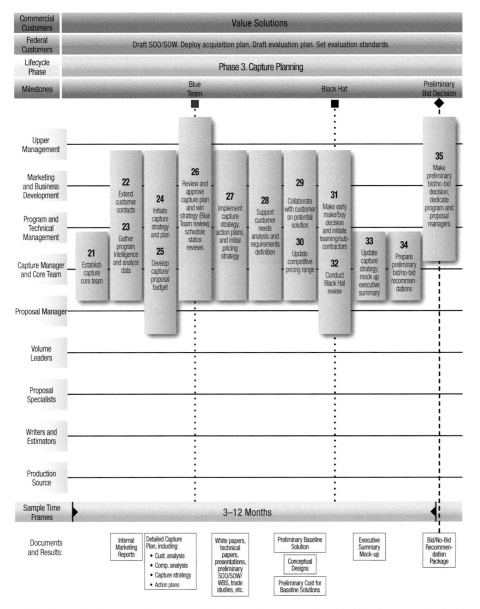

Figure 11. Phase 3: Capture Planning. *The focus of capture planning is to implement winning strategies to capture a specific business opportunity by influencing the customer to prefer your organization and solution before a Request for Proposal (RFP) is released or even written. Work collaboratively with the customer to craft a solution addressing explicit requirements and hot buttons. Gather intelligence about the customer and the competition. Your goal in the over arching capture planning process is to move from a position of "unknown," to "known," and ultimately "preferred." Phase 3 leads to a preliminary Bid Decision Gate review.*

21

21
Establish
capture
core team

See Capture Team
Selection and
Management, *Capture
Guide.*

Establish capture core team

Begin by selecting and naming the core capture team triumvirate, depicted in figure 12. Note that the capture manager, program manager, and proposal manager designations are roles, not necessarily positions, and these roles are often part-time depending upon the size and maturity of the opportunity.

The size of the core team reflects the complexity of the opportunity and the size of the proposal. The core team on a small opportunity might be one person working part time. On larger opportunities, the capture manager often must fill the program and proposal manager roles until individuals are identified and assigned to those roles.

The designation *capture manager* implies a capture team will be formed. As the capture plan is developed, individuals will be added from internal functional departments and potentially from teaming organizations.

Wrap rates refer to rates, which include other costs in addition to labor costs.

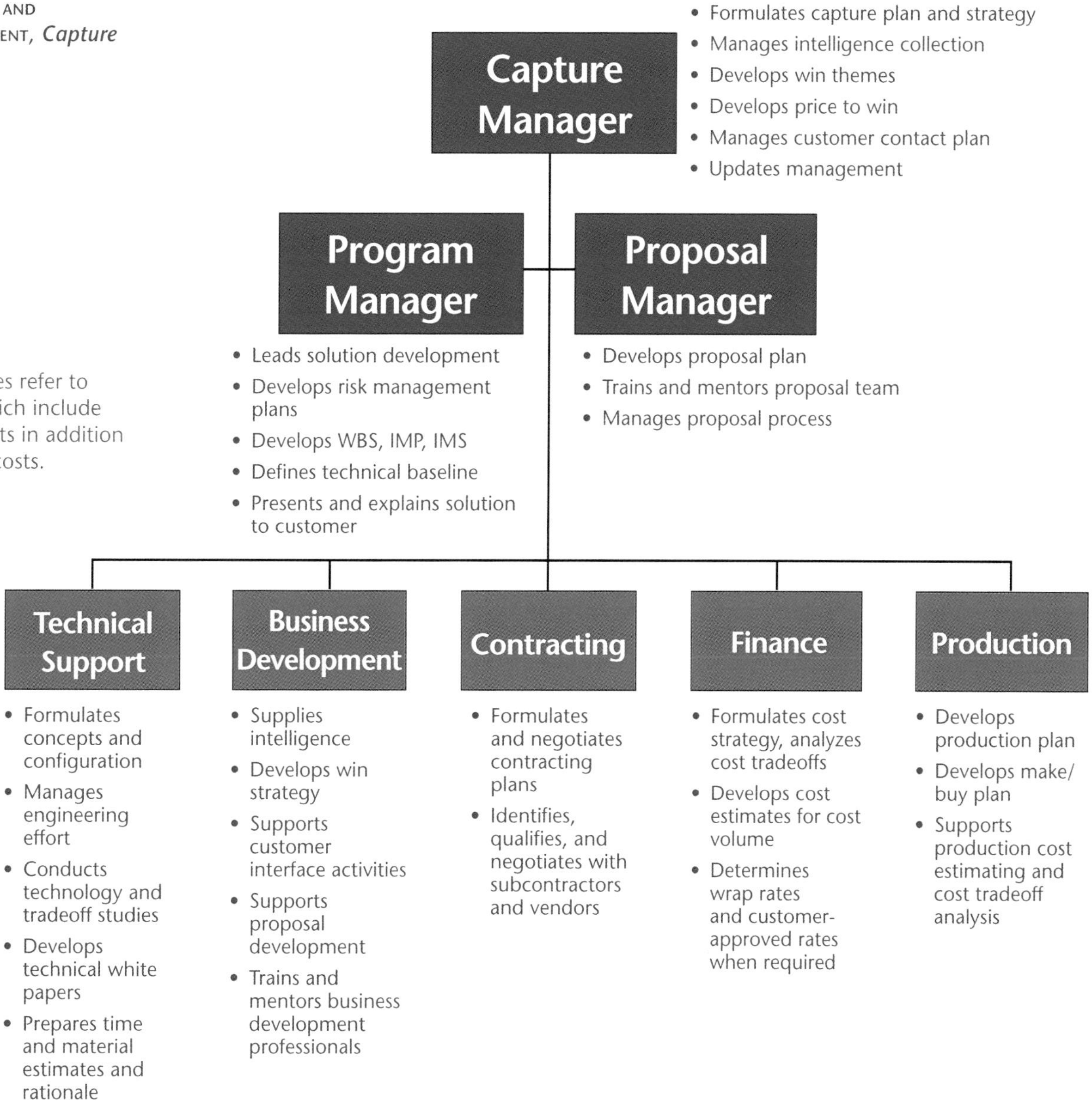

Capture Manager
- Formulates capture plan and strategy
- Manages intelligence collection
- Develops win themes
- Develops price to win
- Manages customer contact plan
- Updates management

Program Manager
- Leads solution development
- Develops risk management plans
- Develops WBS, IMP, IMS
- Defines technical baseline
- Presents and explains solution to customer

Proposal Manager
- Develops proposal plan
- Trains and mentors proposal team
- Manages proposal process

Technical Support
- Formulates concepts and configuration
- Manages engineering effort
- Conducts technology and tradeoff studies
- Develops technical white papers
- Prepares time and material estimates and rationale

Business Development
- Supplies intelligence
- Develops win strategy
- Supports customer interface activities
- Supports proposal development
- Trains and mentors business development professionals

Contracting
- Formulates and negotiates contracting plans
- Identifies, qualifies, and negotiates with subcontractors and vendors

Finance
- Formulates cost strategy, analyzes cost tradeoffs
- Develops cost estimates for cost volume
- Determines wrap rates and customer-approved rates when required

Production
- Develops production plan
- Develops make/buy plan
- Supports production cost estimating and cost tradeoff analysis

Figure 12. The Business Development Opportunity Triumvirate. *Win rates improve when the capture, program, and proposal manager roles are balanced and integrated. Notionally, the program manager owns the solution, typical when selling services. When the solution involves complex technical systems design and development, a technical lead might join or supplant the program manager on the capture core team.*

22 Extend customer contacts

22
Extend customer contacts

See CUSTOMER FOCUSED CAPTURE SKILLS AND TACTICS, PERSUASION, *Capture Guide.*

Throughout this phase, senior management and the core team try to get as much information from their customer contacts as possible.

Depending upon the selling environment, customer contacts are often restricted, so contact, meet, and collaborate as early as possible. The earlier and more collaborative your efforts, the greater your understanding and potential influence on the customer's requirements. Often government customers are willing to share information, but they worry about perceptions of favoritism. Business-to-business customers are generally more open to ongoing discussions.

Learn as much as possible about your customer and individuals in the customer organization before contacting them. Customers are impatient with sellers who fail to do their homework, seeing them as time-wasters. Review your business development and marketing database, account plans, lessons learned reviews from prior programs with this customer, and publicly available data on the web.

23 Gather program intelligence and analyze data

23
Gather program intelligence and analyze data

Review the various capture planning templates included in the MODEL DOCUMENTS, *Capture Guide.*

A capture triumvirate has no substitute for good program intelligence. The more the capture triumvirate knows about the customer's program, key issues, and biases, the more persuasive your capture planning positioning activities. Ask key questions before the bid request is prepared, requirements are defined, and RFP is released.

Listed below are typical business intelligence questions. Add better, more specific questions as you gather the program and customer intelligence required to initially prepare and repeatedly update your capture plan. Review the account plan, if available, and your capture template. Determining what you do not know is often more important than what you know.

- What type of program is it?
- How real is the program?
- Does the customer have budget cuts looming on the horizon?
- Does the customer have a history of project cancellations?
- Has the customer ever sent out "feeler" RFPs, RFIs, or tenders? Are in-house customer organizations potential competitors?
- What is your history with this customer?
- Will the customer specify the type of bidders (for example, disadvantaged, minority, or small-business requirement)?
- Who is the Source Selection Authority (SSA)?
- Who is the program manager?
- Who are the evaluators?

- Do you have any enemies in the customer's shop?
- Do you have any biases to overcome?
- Are there any legislative or regulatory issues regarding this program? Would organizational conflict of interest issues preclude pursuing this opportunity for a future, larger, and more strategic opportunity?
- Has the program been budgeted?
- What is the budget? What portion of the budget is typically held back for management overheads, risks, or other factors? What is the probable price to compete?
- Is the customer cost-sensitive?
- Is there an incumbent?
- Have the competitors had problems with overruns?
- Is cost or capability a more important consideration in awarding the contract?
- What type of contract will it be (i.e., cost plus, fixed price, etc.)?
- If this procurement is a U.S. government "best value" award, will it be under the Lowest Price Technically Acceptable (LPTA) or other trade-off process definitions and guidelines?

Documents and Results

- Internal marketing reports include reports on markets, customers, and competitors; account plans; and lessons learned reports.

24

24

Initiate capture
strategy
and plan

See CAPTURE PLANNING,
CAPTURE STRATEGY,
PRICING TO WIN, *and*
CAPTURE PLAN TEMPLATES
and CAPTURE PLANS in
MODEL DOCUMENTS,
Capture Guide.

Initiate capture strategy and plan

Within the business development planning process, the capture plan is the first plan focused on a specific opportunity target. Most focus on a single purchase, but some focus on linked opportunity targets.

The most important elements of the capture plan are your capture strategy and the associated tactical actions that your team will take to implement that strategy. Balance your capture strategy by focusing equally on your technical, management, and pricing approaches. Too often sellers focus on technical and management aspects, ignoring pricing or treating it as a costing and margining issue.

The capture plan details exactly what you will do to capture the business. It must be concise and specific, stating who will do what and when they will do it. Objectives should be specific and quantified, if possible, so progress can be assessed regularly and adjustments made.

Capture plans are living documents. To support collaborative activities and simplify repeated updates, capture plans might be in text, presentation, or web-browser formats. Web-browser formats offer significant advantages:

- Easy to collaboratively develop, share, and document data in a single location.

- Senior managers can easily monitor progress, updates, and activity.

- Most contributors have a collaboration tool installed as an organizational standard.

- Security on these tools is relatively robust.

Capture templates are seldom completed in order because information does not become available in that order. Use capture plan templates to prompt you to seek relevant data. As the customer moves toward release of the bid request, information will change and become more specific. Use the process shown in figure 13 to create and implement your capture plan.

The capture plan is the central tool used in the capture planning phase, as illustrated in figure 14, and is the basis for gate review briefings and decisions. Briefing from a current capture plan eliminates the need to prepare separate briefing materials.

Capture plans are the basis for the proposal management plan and subsequent proposal efforts. The capture plan is shared with the proposal team to align capture strategies and tactics with supporting proposal strategies and tactics.

Documents and Results

- Detailed capture plan, including:
  - Customer analysis
  - Competitive analysis
  - Capture strategy
  - Action plans

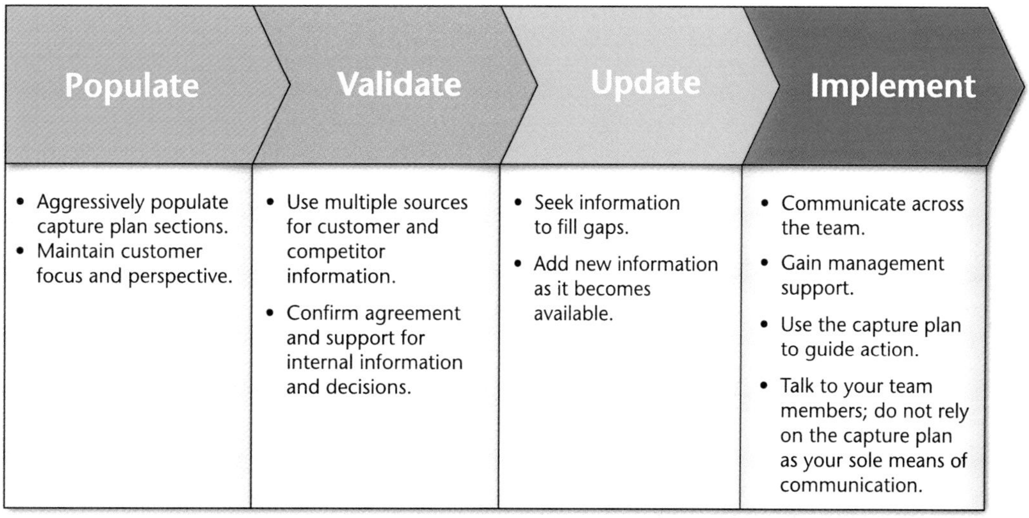

Populate	Validate	Update	Implement
• Aggressively populate capture plan sections. • Maintain customer focus and perspective.	• Use multiple sources for customer and competitor information. • Confirm agreement and support for internal information and decisions.	• Seek information to fill gaps. • Add new information as it becomes available.	• Communicate across the team. • Gain management support. • Use the capture plan to guide action. • Talk to your team members; do not rely on the capture plan as your sole means of communication.

Figure 13. Iteratively Develop Your Capture Plan. *Keep your capture plan current and correct by repeatedly updating the content. Populate—complete what you think you know; validate—check and confirm; update—add and correct data; then, implement.*

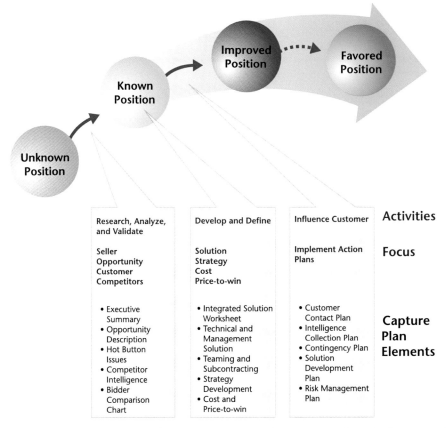

Figure 14. Aligning the Capture Planning Process to the Capture Plan. *In the over arching capture planning process, you seek to move from positions of "unknown," to "known," and then to an "improved position." If highly successful, you may be able to move into a "preferred position" prior to release of a formal solicitation. Elements of the capture plan are matched to this iterative process by phase. Specific content of your capture plans will vary depending on the opportunity, your organization, and the value of the opportunity to your organization.*

25

25
Develop capture/ proposal budget

See CAPTURE SCHEDULING, *Capture Guide.*

Develop capture/proposal budget

A positive pursuit decision includes the explicit approval of capture planning expenditures through to the Preliminary Bid Decision Gate review. However, you need to prepare a complete capture planning budget, which includes proposal preparation costs. Capture costs might include:

- R&D
- Positioning visits to customer
- Demonstrations
- Advertising and recruitment
- Time for telephone calls, faxes, letters, and e-mail
- Search for teaming partners
- Internal briefings, management reviews, and white papers
- Monthly status/progress reports preparation and delivery

Proposal costs might include:

- Planning resources
- Design or engineering development
- Customer demonstrations
- Internal and external presentations
- Proposal development personnel, facilities, and equipment
- Production and reproduction
- Oral proposal preparation and rehearsal
- Language translations

Most capture managers set initial capture planning and proposal preparation budgets based on historic costs associated with the value of the opportunity. Adjust your initial budget according to the probable procurement schedule, capture tactics planned, and resources available for the pursuit.

Many costs are hidden. For most organizations, the actual costs for capture planning and proposal preparation are significantly higher than the budgeted costs.

26 Review and approve capture plan and win strategy (Blue Team review); schedule status reviews

26
Review and approve capture plan and win strategy (Blue Team review); schedule status reviews

See Color Team Reviews, *Capture Guide.*

Schedule a Blue Team review of your draft capture plan and win strategy. The Blue Team reviews the initial capture plan to evaluate your knowledge of the customer and opportunity, provides guidance on your potential solution, and recommends strategic actions you can take to position your organization as the customer's preferred choice. From this point forward, the capture team should follow the agreed win strategy unless evidence surfaces that it is not making you competitive.

Ideally, Blue Team members and the team facilitator are independent of the capture team and knowledgeable about the customer, customer needs, competitors, competitors' solutions, and your organization and solution.

Figure 15 lists desired outputs. Schedule a second Blue Team review if the Black Hat Team review, Step 32, prompts you to significantly modify your capture strategy or solution.

Milestones

- Blue Team

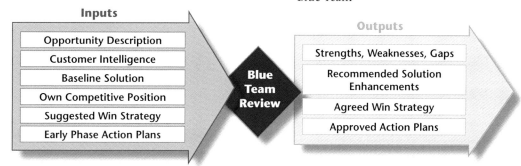

Figure 15. Blue Team Inputs and Outputs. *Blue Team members identify strengths, weaknesses, and gaps, and recommend improvements. They affirm the early actions of the capture team or advise them on modifications to their plans. They do not allocate or withdraw resources; the capture manager and executive team will make those decisions later.*

27 Implement capture strategy, action plans, and initial pricing strategy

27
Implement capture strategy, action plans, and initial pricing strategy

The capture manager, with support from the capture triumvirate, manages implementation tactics, evaluates feedback, assesses progress, and repeatedly updates implementation tactics.

Because the objective of capture planning is to influence the customer to prefer your organization and solution, balance capture planning and implementation. Persuasion takes time and repeated interaction and collaboration with the customer. Persuading a group of

individuals in the customer organization with different hot button issues requires coordinated actions by individuals in the selling organization that repeatedly deliver aligned, customer-focused messages.

Documents and Results

- White papers, technical papers, presentations, preliminary Statement of Objectives (SOO)/Statement of Work (SOW)/Work Breakdown Structure (WBS), trade studies, etc.

28 Support customer needs analysis and requirements definition

28
Support customer needs analysis and requirements definition

During the capture effort, BD and the capture team work with the customer to refine needs and identify specific requirements. When you clearly understand the customer's needs and specific requirements, you are more likely to be on target with your proposal. When a Statement of Objectives (SOO) is substituted

for a detailed Statement of Work (SOW), being as specific as possible regarding customer objectives, hot button issues, and requirements will help you propose a more competitive solution.

29

**29
Collaborate
with customer
on potential
solution**

See PERSUASION *and* PRESENTATIONS TO CUSTOMERS, *Capture Guide.*

Collaborate with customer on potential solution

One of the most powerful positioning tools for any organization is collaborative effort with a customer as it assesses and values alternative solutions. Through collaborative effort, identify, understand, and validate customer hot button issues and requirements while pre-selling your solution. Collaboration builds the customer's confidence in your organization and solution.

Avoid surprising your customer with a new solution in your proposal. Most customers perceive new solutions as higher risk and solutions that are developed collaboratively as lower risk.

Documents and Results

- Preliminary baseline solution
- Conceptual designs

30

**30
Update
competitive
pricing range**

See COSTING *and* PRICING TO WIN, *Capture Guide.*

Update competitive pricing range

Capture teams should not develop solutions in isolation, but in conjunction with pricing. Early in a pursuit, a preliminary price to compete helps place evolving solutions within a range the customer can afford. That range is bounded on the low side by the minimum price the customer finds credible and on the high side by the customer's addressable budget for the procurement, i.e., the amount the customer can pay after allocating necessary management and overhead funding.

The customer's price and budget expectations might also be influenced by independent cost estimates (ICE) or internal *should-cost* analyses, which factor in changes in market conditions, technology, and program complexity.

Customers generally define, or can be helped to define, a minimum acceptable capability. Similarly, they seldom buy a solution beyond the maximum justifiable capability.

Together, these price and capability limits define a winning price window, the region of a price and capability trade space that bound the customer's notion of best value. Figure 16 illustrates how the conceptual winning price window narrows over time as the customer's understanding of needs, available solutions, and funding improves.

As your capture team collects and analyzes competitive intelligence, develop and iteratively refine a price to win, considering not only the customer's winning price window, but competitors' likely offers. Your estimate of the winning price becomes the position in the winning price window that maximizes your win probability. This process of developing and implementing strategies to achieve the price to win is called pricing to win.

To develop estimates of competitors' positions in the winning price window, consider their probable capabilities, strategies, and tactics.

Focus on competitors' prior, successful strategies, as they are likely to repeat successful strategies. Pricing-to-win professionals maintain that focusing on competitors' prior strategies is more predictive and useful than focusing on their prior rates and exact bid prices.

Understanding the customer's buying position or interest also helps zero in on a price that can win. Such insights can often help you understand and anticipate customer behavior. Buyers typically exhibit one of three styles:

- Budget-limited buyers cannot afford the capability they want, will be disappointed, but will spend all available funds.
- Capability-satisfed buyers know their requirements and will purchase a solution that meets their needs at the lowest possible cost. They will resist up-selling.
- Best-value buyers balance price and capability according to their perceptions of value. They constitute the majority of customers in structured markets for complex sales. In a climate of severe budget restrictions, customers are increasingly defining best value as a low price.

In U.S. federal procurements, the Federal Acquisition Regulation (FAR) defines two best value options: lowest price technically acceptable (LPTA) and trade-off process. If LPTA is used, then your solution set should be marginally technically acceptable at the lowest price and margin that you can accept.

Note that a price to win does not exist in isolation. It is always an intersection of price and capability.

Documents and Results

- Preliminary cost for baseline solutions

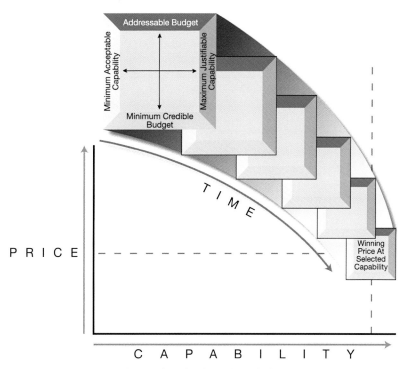

Figure 16. Winning Price Window. *The winning price window narrows over time as customers learn their needs and what budgets and solutions are available.*

31

31
Make early make/buy decision and initiate teaming/sub-contractors

See TEAMING, *Capture Guide*.

Make early make/buy decision and initiate teaming/subcontractors

Cost, capability, and quality depend upon the source, whether internal or external resources. If internal, determine which division or location. If external, identify the vendor, subcontractor, or teaming partner. When working with external resources, determine if you want an exclusive relationship and their degree of involvement in the capture planning effort. Figure 17 lists make/buy and teaming considerations.

The first consideration listed is critical. The capture manager must validate that prospective teammates are preferred or at least acceptable to the customer and anticipated evaluators. An early decision gives you more time to influence the customer's view of teammates and your entire team.

The earlier you can make these decisions, the earlier you can bound your cost, price, and capability trade-offs.

FACTOR	CONSIDERATIONS
Enhance team strength	Offset weaknesses; add capabilities or discriminators; add key personnel; current reputation with customer; small, disadvantaged, minority, or economic development zone business status to meet customer-restricted bidding requirements
Complementary roles and responsibilities	Avoid duplication of roles; conflicts with other contracts; potential; work shares for proposal and program
Augment capture capabilities	Agree on lead; sell integrated team; political influence
Enhance intellectual property	Guidelines for information and technology transfer
Logistics implications	Travel; co-location; technology standards; archives; compatible processes, values, and systems
Mutual protection	Binding legal and nondisclosure agreements; termination provisions; financial contributions; risk assumptions

Figure 17. Teaming Considerations. *Teaming decisions are important and often have repercussions beyond the immediate opportunity. Weigh the factors and implications when choosing partners and reaching teaming agreements.*

32

32
Conduct
Black Hat
review

See COLOR TEAM REVIEWS *and* PRICING TO WIN, *Capture Guide*.

Ideally, pricing to win analysts supply comprehensive competitive analysis information to Black Hat reviewers. If not, then this responsibility falls to Black Hat reviewers by default and often incorporates greater bias.

Conduct Black Hat review

Black Hat Team members are experts on the customer and competitors. They try to anticipate competitors' strategies and solutions and test the soundness of your strategy and solution.

Black Hat Teams prepare capture plans for each major competitor or major types of competitors. They outline competitors' probable solutions and strategies based on their knowledge of the market, the customer, and competitors' prior strategies and capabilities.

Conduct multiple Black Hat Team reviews when prompted by major changes in the requirements, competition, or competitors' probable solutions. Conduct simplified Black Hat reviews for smaller competitions.

Conduct a *technical* Black Hat review as a subset, focused on outlining competitors' baseline solutions in sufficient detail to estimate their probable bid prices.

Figure 18 shows the inputs and outputs of the Black Hat review. The ideal Black Hat review

outcome is to credibly answer the following types of questions:

- How do you shape the game?
- What are the competitors' likely strategies?
- How do you stack up against the competition in technical capabilities, price, risk, and past performance?
- What are the competitors' strengths and weaknesses?
- What issues do you *ghost*?
- Whom does the customer prefer?
- If you are not the incumbent, how do you unseat them?
- If you *are* the incumbent, how do you retain your position?
- How do you become *the* competitor to beat? Can you achieve a favored position?
- How can you counteract the competitors' marketing efforts?

Milestones

- Black Hat

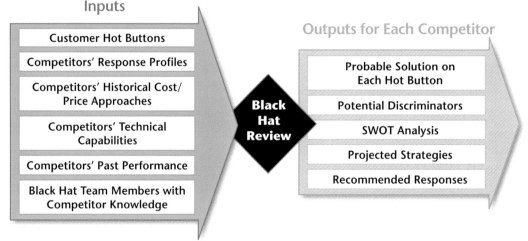

Figure 18. Black Hat Review. *Divide Black Hat review members into teams representing various competitors. Using competitive response profiles, estimate each competitor's most plausible solution to the customer's needs. Ask each team to develop the likely capture plan for the assigned competitor. Form a technical design subset to develop competitors' baseline solutions in sufficient detail to estimate their probable bid prices.*

33

33
Update
capture
strategy; mock
up executive
summary

Update capture strategy; mock up executive summary

Revisit the customer's hot buttons and the probable competitor list and update your capture strategy. Incorporate new competitors; changes in customer perceptions, hot button issues, and requirements; and market and technology shifts.

Update the technical, management, and pricing aspects of your capture strategy. Remember that your price to win is a trade-off between price and capability that offers the best value to this customer.

See Executive Summary, *Capture Guide*.

Jump start the proposal effort by developing a mock-up of the Executive Summary. Using the customer-focused approach shown in figure 19, align the customer's hot button issues with elements of your solution. If you cannot link an element of your solution to a hot button issue, eliminate that element or develop a strategy to influence the customer to value that element.

Using the customer hot button organization places the focus on the customer. Your final proposal Executive Summary might subsequently be realigned with the evaluation criteria, but the key content and customer focus are retained.

Documents and Results

- Executive summary mockup

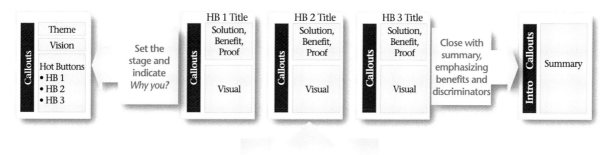

Figure 19. **Hot Button Executive Summary.** *An executive summary organized according to the customer's hot buttons is a remarkably effective communication tool. Use your executive summary mockup to brief internal management and subsequent proposal team.*

---

34 Prepare preliminary bid/no-bid recommendations

34
Prepare preliminary bid/no-bid recommen-dations

See Decision Gate Reviews, Pricing to Win, *and* Model Documents, *Capture Guide*.

The Preliminary Bid Decision Gate review is precipitated by the customer's decision to seek bids.

Pre-define Preliminary Bid Decision Gate review inputs and outputs for your organization, but scale and adapt your requirements to the market, selling environment, customer, and competitive situation. The most direct solution is to define the capture plan elements and desired level of detail required for this gate review. Your updated capture plan should suffice for this review and, if current, preparation is minimal.

Sample questions for building a bid/no-bid question list

Adapt the following lists of questions to your organization and selling environment. Most of these questions should be incorporated in your capture planning template. If not, add them as relevant.

Assess the customer

- What agency or departments are involved in the buying process? Who are the main contacts?
- Are they reliable? Do you like to do business with them? Do they like to do business with you?

- How does the customer view the incumbent, if one exists?
- What are the parts, phases, and sequences involved in the procurement?
- How have you been involved in and influenced customer objectives, requirements, or specifications? Who is involved? How?
- Who are the key decision makers and influencers? Who are the key people in other agencies, government bodies, consulting organizations, or industry locations?
- What are the internal customer politics, policies, or biases that might influence requirements and selection decisions?
- What else do you need to know about this customer and this procurement?
- What is the need that is causing the customer to seek a solution? What value does the customer place on solving or alleviating this need?

Assess capabilities and objectives

- Why do you want this business?
- Is this procurement in line with the business plans and with your projections?
- Do you have the physical resources and capability to pursue it and to handle the job if you win? What more might be required? Can you bid it and make money? If not, is there still a compelling reason to bid?

- Who are your key management, technical, and other personnel? Are they available? Are they known and liked by this customer?
- What unique or special advantages do you bring to such a procurement?
- What teaming or contracting arrangements might be required? Are such arrangements practical?
- What is your track record on similar activities with this client? With similar clients?
- Who might be your program manager?
- On what strengths would you win this procurement? On what weaknesses might you lose it?
- How have you influenced the operational requirements or project/design requirements?

Assess the competitors

- Who is the incumbent?
- Who might be competitors?
- Can you team to preempt a formidable competitor team?
- Who has a history of successful work with this customer? Can you compete?
- What are the strengths and weaknesses of each of your competitors?
- What are the traditional bidding/pricing practices for each of your competitors? When they win, what is the key factor? What prior successful pricing and solutioning strategies are they likely to repeat?
- What are the long-term competitive implications for the winners and losers of this bid?
- What are the "political" forces now operating or surrounding this procurement? Who cares on Capitol Hill? Are you in a politically favorable position to win? Is someone else?
- What public relations, advertising, and promotion work might be needed to highlight your strengths and overcome competitors' strengths?

Assess the financial opportunity

- What is the dollar value of the procurement? Who knows this information?
- What profits/benefits can you expect? Have you prepared a business case?

- Do you gain some long-term capability/capacity that will position your organization for future earnings?
- How does this customer typically structure their buys?
- How do they conduct procurements? What are their contracting practices?
- Does the funding exist? Are different types of funds budgeted, such as capital versus operating costs? What is the timing? What will be required for the funding to be allocated? Will the funding stay in place over the life of the project?
- Do you have the B&P money to pursue it?
- Can you meet the customer's requirements? At what cost?
- What is your chance of winning? What would it cost you to win?
- On what basis (cost) will the procurement be won or lost? Are you strong here? How about your competition?
- Will the customer require warranties? Offsets? Investments? Performance bonds? Liquidated damages?
- Is payment subject to revenues generated?

Define the opportunity

- Exactly what is the customer requesting at this time? How firm is this?
- What is the scope of the project at this time? Will it change?
- What is the time period for the procurement? For the project? Is this typical? Reasonable?
- How does this fit into your long-term business plan?
- What are the procurement terms and requirements? What is typical for this customer?
- What office and person are leading the effort for the customer? Can you work compatibly with them over the life of the contract?
- Will it happen as projected? What is your experience?
- When will the bid request be issued?
- When will the procurement begin and end?
- Can you meet the requirements now, without major retooling, hiring, or change? How significant are those requirements you cannot meet now?

35

35
Make preliminary bid/no-bid decision; dedicate program and proposal managers

Make preliminary bid/no-bid decision; dedicate program and proposal managers

Your objective for the Preliminary Bid Decision Gate review is to determine if your capture activities have improved your position sufficiently to justify planning and preparing a proposal.

Invite senior managers who have a stake in the effort due to their management responsibilities, control of resources, market expertise, or service and product expertise. Objectively review the positive and negative aspects of continuing or ending the pursuit. Ground decisions on facts rather than subjective opinions.

If you decide to advance, identify and assign a proposal manager and program manager, if not done previously. Often the capture manager identifies the preferred key core team personnel, but they have not yet been assigned to support the pursuit.

See DECISION GATE REVIEWS, *Capture Guide.*

Some organizations assign program and proposal manager roles to one individual. Occasionally, due to program size or corporate resources, this may be necessary. However, for most large programs, assign different people.

Program manager and proposal manager are distinct roles. The program manager is the single individual on the capture team responsible for delivering a successful solution to the customer that results in quality past performance reviews and additional work. The program manager is program- and delivery-team focused, frequently reviewing resumes for program personnel; structuring the program organization, functions, and WBS; resolving teaming relationships and agreements; and coordinating with the customer and subcontractors. The program manager needs to be separate in order to be the *sanity check* on what's going into the proposal.

The proposal manager is focused on proposal development, including maintaining schedules, coordinating inputs, conducting reviews, implementing strategy, and resolving internal problems.

If you delay selecting the program manager, you delay solution development and pricing. When work begins on the proposal before the baseline solution is defined, the solution tends to be marginally compliant, marginally responsive, unpersuasive, generic, and seller focused. Disconnects between different aspects of the solution described in the proposal also impact pricing and risk.

A well-conceived and executed capture plan prepares the proposal team to write a successful proposal. The capture manager's goal is to arrive at final RFP release in a favored position with the customer; with winning baseline solutions in technical, management, past performance, and cost or price areas; and confirmation that the capture strategy and proposal strategy are approved and aligned.

Increase your win probability and reduce business capture costs by incorporating or adapting capture plan elements into the proposal management plan, as shown in figure 20.

Milestones

- Preliminary bid decision

Documents and Results

- Bid/no-bid recommendation package

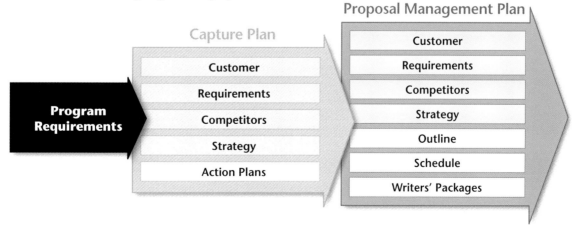

Figure 20. Capture Plan Evolution. *For large proposals, or proposals with many teaming partners, the proposal manager might package essential planning documents in a Proposal Management Plan (PMP). In such cases, much of the background information from the capture plan can be reused. Alternatively, the same information is shared on a secure, web-accessible site. The proposal manager adds proposal-specific information, including the outline, schedule, and individual writers' instruction packages. Note that when the capture manager engages proposal support, capture planning, proposal planning, and proposal preparation continue in parallel.*

Proposal Planning before writing saves more time than it takes. In parallel with ongoing capture planning activities, plan and validate your proposal plan before you begin writing new material or tailoring reuse material.

Focus on three proposal planning activities:

- Migrate data from the capture plan to the proposal management plan
- Extend the capture strategy into the proposal strategy
- Refine the solution and price to win

If you lack a capture plan, capture strategy, solution, and price to win, winning will be difficult with too much to do in too little time. Before the bid request arrives (see figure 21), proactively assemble and task a proposal core team to prepare a proposal management plan focused on the three proposal planning activities.

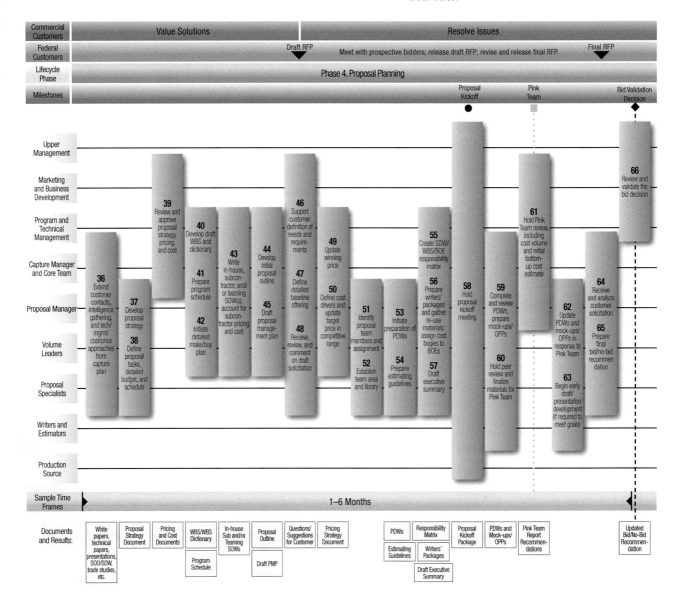

Figure 21. Phase 4: Proposal Planning. *In Phase 4, you plan how your team will write a winning proposal upon release of a bid request. Developing a solution, price to win, and proposal strategy, and recruiting proposal developers after the bid request is released divert resources and management focus from preparing a winning proposal. The precipitating customer event marking the end of proposal planning is the release of the final bid request, leading to your Bid Validation Decision Gate review.*

36

36
Extend
customer
contacts,
intelligence
gathering,
and tech/
mgmt/
cost/price
approaches
from
capture
plan

Extend customer contacts, intelligence gathering, and tech/mgmt/cost/price approaches from capture plan

Extend customer contacts and intelligence gathering as early as possible. In many markets, customers restrict direct communications with sellers after the bid request is released, so exploit this valuable opportunity.

Marketing, sales, and field representatives; technical and management people; and other members of the capture planning team might be involved in a series of on site visits coordinated by the capture manager. Use these visits to better understand the customer's needs, hot button issues, and views on potential solutions and requirements.

Offer expert technical and program assistance to help the customer value alternative solutions and refine requirements before the final bid request is issued. Your objective is to influence the customer to prefer your solution and organization.

Documents and Results
- White papers, technical papers, presentations, SOO/SOW, trade studies, etc.

37

37
Develop
proposal
strategy

Develop proposal strategy

Extend the capture strategy into the proposal strategy. If your capture and proposal messages are aligned, they are more credible and your win probability increases. Proposal strategy consists of a series of statements that state your point or position and how you plan to make that point in your proposal.

Translate capture strategy statements into proposal strategy statements, and then assign each statement to one or more proposal sections via the writers' packages, as shown in figure 22.

Documents and Results
- Proposal strategy document

See Strategy *and* Storyboards and Mockups, *Proposal Guide.*

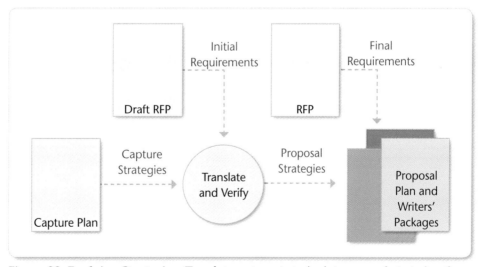

Figure 22. Evolving Strategies. *Translate capture strategies into proposal strategies, then assign each proposal strategy to one or more proposal sections via the writers' packages. Compare the capture plan, draft RFP, and final RFP to see if the customer's requirements have changed and your assumptions remain correct.*

38

38
Define proposal tasks, detailed budget, and schedule

See PRODUCTION, PROPOSAL MANAGEMENT PLAN, *and* SCHEDULING; *Proposal Guide.*

Define proposal tasks, detailed budget, and schedule

Proposal managers develop the proposal project schedule to manage proposal contributors within a defined process. Proposal managers, core team members, and section writers use the schedule to manage themselves and others.

Deadlines drive proposal schedules, with surprisingly minimal influence from the size of the tasks. Use the scheduling recommendations in figure 23 and the standards in figure 24 to prepare your proposal schedule until you have developed your own recommendations and metrics.

The guidelines in figure 23 summarize key recommendations for the proposal manager. Figure 24 offers guidelines for estimating the time required for various proposal writing tasks.

SCHEDULING RECOMMENDATIONS	
Schedule backwards	Schedule proposal submission first. Next, schedule key milestones. Adjust timing as tasks are added.
Reserve contingency time	Allow time for unanticipated problems.
Maximize parallel tasks	Avoid bottlenecks by scheduling many tasks simultaneously.
Estimate realistically	Use time standards below—or those developed within your organization—to ensure adequate time is allowed for critical tasks.
Resource optimally	Conserve budget by assigning start and end dates for each task. Avoid assigning personnel for the duration of the proposal to minimize *marching army* costs.
Use standard work periods	Except on very short schedules, leave weekends and holidays free. These days may be needed later for schedule recovery.
Plan for production	Do not force the production staff to absorb others' delays.
Plan for reviews	Allow adequate time to complete reviews and incorporate comments.
Manage to the schedule	Develop recovery plans whenever task completions slip.

Figure 23. Scheduling Proposals. *Setting a schedule will help you allocate your resources effectively and help you foresee and respond to challenges before they arise. At this stage, your proposal schedule is a plan that will likely be adjusted when the RFP is released.*

Proposal task estimating standards compare poorly across organizations. However, by developing metrics, you will improve productivity as contributors strive to meet your internal standards.

TASK-ESTIMATING STANDARDS	
Task	*Time Standard*
Write new material	4 pages per day
Revise text or edit for content	8–10 pages per day
Proofreading	20–25 pages per day
Create simple graphic	1–2 hours
Create complex graphic	2–6 hours
Retouch photograph	1–2 hours
Red Teaming	40 pages per day
Desktop publishing	30–60 pages per day

Figure 24. Proposal Scheduling Time Standards. *Adopt these standards as a starting point until you develop more reliable standards. Poor standards lead to poor proposals and potentially late proposals.*

The timeline in figure 25 shows major milestones associated with proposal development, regardless of duration or complexity. Approximate intervals between these milestones are shown for three illustrative examples:

- Short, quick-turn proposals (10 days)
- Typical schedules (30 days)
- Extended preparation cycles (90 days)

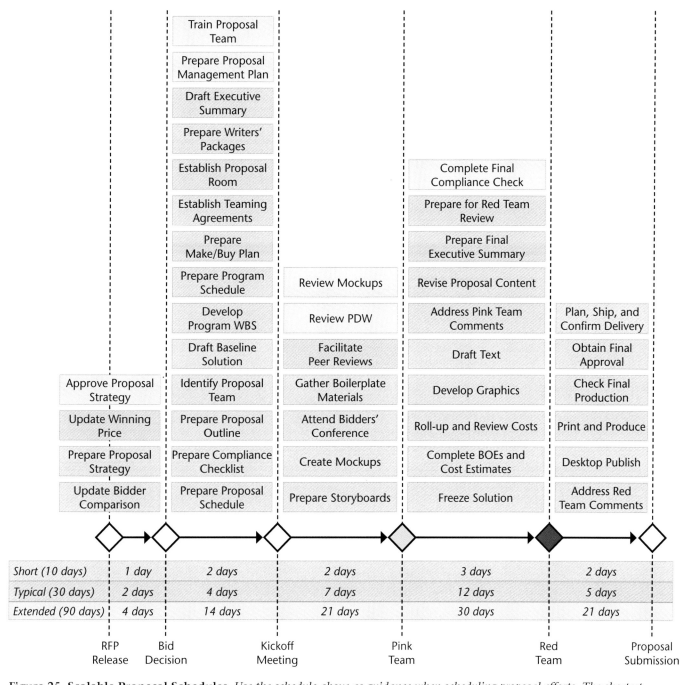

| | Train Proposal Team |
| Prepare Proposal Management Plan |
| Draft Executive Summary |
| Prepare Writers' Packages |
Establish Proposal Room		Complete Final Compliance Check
Establish Teaming Agreements		Prepare for Red Team Review
Prepare Make/Buy Plan		Prepare Final Executive Summary
Prepare Program Schedule	Review Mockups	Revise Proposal Content
Develop Program WBS	Review PDW	Address Pink Team Comments	Plan, Ship, and Confirm Delivery
Draft Baseline Solution	Facilitate Peer Reviews	Draft Text	Obtain Final Approval
Approve Proposal Strategy	Identify Proposal Team	Gather Boilerplate Materials	Develop Graphics	Check Final Production
Update Winning Price	Prepare Proposal Outline	Attend Bidders' Conference	Roll-up and Review Costs	Print and Produce
Prepare Proposal Strategy	Prepare Compliance Checklist	Create Mockups	Complete BOEs and Cost Estimates	Desktop Publish
Update Bidder Comparison	Prepare Proposal Schedule	Prepare Storyboards	Freeze Solution	Address Red Team Comments

Short (10 days)	1 day	2 days	2 days	3 days	2 days	
Typical (30 days)	2 days	4 days	7 days	12 days	5 days	
Extended (90 days)	4 days	14 days	21 days	30 days	21 days	

| RFP Release | Bid Decision | Kickoff Meeting | Pink Team | Red Team | Proposal Submission |

Figure 25. Scalable Proposal Schedules. *Use the schedule above as guidance when scheduling proposal efforts. The shortest schedules, such as for task order responses, include essential tasks. As the proposal preparation time lengthens, tasks and reviews are added. Large system acquisition schedules often include proposal team training; detailed solution, strategy, and price-to-win reviews; and multiple Pink and Red Team reviews. The activities in green and blue are additive to the shorter list of activities in gray, based on the time available. Your proposal schedule is a crucial proposal development and management tool. Insert major tasks and reviews in an initial milestone schedule. Then add detail in an inch-stone schedule, including the date and time to start and complete sub-tasks.*

If you lack a draft bid request, estimate the submittal date and time based on prior, similar bid requests issued by this customer. Adjust when the draft and final bid requests are issued. While bid requests are often issued late, do not assume that the submittal date will also be extended. Regard extensions as "bonus time" that you can use to polish your proposal.

Follow these guidelines to construct a flowchart:

- Study the generic Shipley 96-step proposal development flowchart and adjust it to match your proposal process.

- Question every step, eliminating non-applicable steps.

- Construct a similar proposal development flowchart. For small, rapid-response proposals, simplify the schedule. For larger proposals, add steps and consider using project management software.

- Identify the decision gate and color team reviews required by your senior management for this type of proposal. Use different symbols to represent tasks and reviews.

- Do not schedule weekends; use them for catch-up days if personnel get behind.

- Make the flowchart in two sizes:
  - Small ones that team members can hang in their offices
  - A large one to hang in the proposal room to refer to during stand-up meetings

- Review the schedule at daily proposal stand-up meetings, with emphasis on near-term inch-stone tasks for that day and week.

39

39
Review and approve proposal strategy, pricing, and cost

See REVIEWS, *Proposal Guide.*

Review and approve proposal strategy, pricing, and cost

Gather an independent team of people, including managers, to review, validate, and suggest improvements to your proposal strategy. Ask them to review your technical, management, and pricing solution against the customer's needs and requirements; the alignment with the capture strategy; and competitive focus.

Documents and Results

- Pricing and cost documents
- Develop draft WBS and dictionary

40

40
Develop draft WBS and dictionary

Develop draft WBS and dictionary

Led by the cost volume manager, the proposal core team, including the proposal, technical volume, and management volume managers begins developing the Work Breakdown Structure (WBS) and WBS dictionary. The WBS identifies and links the hardware, services, and data elements of your solution to the supplier. The WBS dictionary defines the hardware, service, and data elements.

If the RFP lacks a WBS, build one. Customers often include a WBS to more easily compare offerors' solutions. Use the customer's WBS, if possible, or plan to justify your deviations.

Prepare the WBS in sufficient detail to cost, schedule, and subcontract accurately. Disclose your WBS at the level you are prepared to report during program execution.

Documents and Results

- WBS/WBS Dictionary

41

41
Prepare program schedule

Prepare program schedule

The core team develops a master program schedule from the strawman RFP, draft RFP, or prior intelligence. The management volume team should also develop an in-house second-tier schedule that shows the timing of each program task.

Writers and estimators need a program schedule to determine task sequence and to place the cost estimate in the appropriate time period. If the RFP requires an Integrated Master Plan (IMP) and Integrated Master Schedule (IMS), identify and assign a specialist for this complex task.

42

42
Initiate detailed make/buy plan

Initiate detailed make/buy plan

As part of the capture plan, the capture manager and program manager outline the make/buy plan and initiate preliminary teaming and subcontracting relationships. Make/buy plans apply to services and products.

In this step, the program manager initiates the detailed make/buy plan for distribution to the proposal developers. Your make/buy decisions affect who describes, costs, and prices the task.

Consider these make/buy questions:

- Which production or service delivery facility is most competitive, produces the best quality, and has the capacity?
- Do you or a vendor have necessary tooling, production equipment, management systems, and trained personnel available?
- Can you tie this to another program to reduce costs?
- Have you made the product or delivered this service before? What is our past performance record? Can it be verified?

Make/buy and teaming considerations are inseparable. Customers often impose work share requirements such as small, minority, or disadvantaged business percentages.

Multinational sales often require production sharing, relating to technology transfer and sources of funds. Some geographic production decisions must be aligned with political considerations—elected officials might link funding approvals to work being placed within their jurisdiction.

The cost volume manager creates a responsibility matrix using the RFP SOW, the WBS, Contract Data Requirements List (CDRL), and the Contract Line Item Numbers (CLINs), if appropriate, to identify department responsibility by task.

In the proposal, all SOW tasks and CLINs must be tied to the WBS. Prepare an SOW/WBS cross-reference matrix to ensure they are parallel and to maintain compatibility between the technical, management, and cost volumes. The SOW/WBS Responsibility Matrix can also be used as a checklist to ensure all RFP requirements are addressed.

43

43
Write in-house, subcon-tractor, and/or teaming SOW(s); account for subcon-tractor pricing and cost

Write in-house, subcontractor, and/or teaming SOW(s); account for subcontractor pricing and cost

The program, technical volume, or management volume manger supervises the development of the in-house, subcontractor, or teaming SOWs. Consider assigning an experienced contracts manager to prepare the teaming SOW, as subcontractors will vie for maximum work shares, often seeking written commitments.

Identify each RFP task, describe what will be done, and who will be responsible to manage and complete the task. The overriding principle is to include all tasks, eliminate overlapping tasks, and define the interfaces among tasks. If not, you will either over- or under-cost tasks and damage your credibility with the customer. Overlapping tasks lead to double costing and defective pricing.

Prepare a subcontractor and/or teaming SOW based on the preliminary make/buy decision, draft WBS, program schedule, and in-house SOW. The subcontractor/teaming SOW defines the tasks and responsibilities of the subcontractors or team members. Most proposal preparation efforts are delayed while waiting for subcontractor and vendor quotes. Early issuance of a detailed subcontractor/teaming SOW will save time and make the complete offer more competitive.

Define all interfaces. Will two product parts fit together? Who pays packaging and freight? Who writes the maintenance manual? Who stocks replacement parts? In service contracts, who does the customer call for repairs? How to bill and get paid? What documentation is required, such as service reports? Incumbents have a major advantage because these details are usually resolved.

Documents and Results

- In-house sub and/or teaming SOWs

44

44
Develop initial proposal outline

See OUTLINING, and STORYBOARDS AND MOCKUPS, Proposal Guide.

Develop initial proposal outline

Adjust how you prepare the proposal outline depending upon the availability of customer guidelines and the importance of the opportunity.

- Outline according to the proposal preparation instructions. These are found in Section L in most U.S. federal RFPs. Find a home within that framework for the requirements in other RFP sections.

- Insert additional topics from the Statement of Work (SOW) or Work Breakdown Structure (WBS), but keep to the basic outline mentioned earlier. (The SOW is found in Section C in a federal RFP.) following the structure of the WBS and SOW. In a performance-based bid request, follow the Statement of Objectives (SOO).

- Incorporate evaluation criteria in the proposal outline.

- When working with a non-U.S. federal bid request, identify similar content and follow a similar outlining process.

- Allocate pages according to evaluation criteria (from Section M of a federal RFP) weights, tempered by the complexity of the material required to address the requirements.

- Reflect the principles of good writing. After setting up volume, chapter, and section titles and sketching out their respective themes, outline the next lower units—the subsections. If outlining sections, list the subsections, and then break down the subsections by topic.

- Designate page limits or guidelines by section and identify potential visual elements by annotating your proposal outline.

If no RFP proposal preparation guidelines exist, follow these outlining suggestions:

- Review the evaluation criteria, SOW, SOO, and customer hot button issues.

- Develop an outline that follows the evaluation criteria, SOW, SOO, or hot button issues.

- Identify where you will discuss risk management, the technical solution, management solution, transition plan, trade studies, and past performance. Insert missing topics, if relevant.

If a draft RFP is not going to be released and this is a *must win*, draft a strawman RFP. Base your strawman RFP on previous RFPs for similar

projects issued by the same organization. Add technical, management, and cost information from capture planning intelligence gathering.

- Focus on four sections that largely define proposal organization, evaluation, contents, and pricing requirements:
  - Proposal organization instructions. Develop an overall topical outline and approximate page limits.
  - Evaluation criteria. Rank and weight probable evaluation criteria. Use the weights to approximate the page allocation by topic.
  - SOW. List and briefly describe probable work tasks, deliverables, and data requirements. Integrate information from prior RFPs and customer visits or web posts.
  - Contract line items that must be priced. Typically, contract line items are listed at a higher level than the tasks and deliverables described in the SOW.

- Revise as necessary.

Extensively annotate the proposal outline to make it an effective proposal management tool. Insert explanatory notes and guidance for proposal developers. The more detailed the annotations, the easier the subsequent transition to Proposal Development Worksheets (PDWs) or storyboards. Consider including the following items:

- Section number
- Relevant RFP section number
- Requirement from the RFP
- Page allocation
- Title
- Owner/developer
- Desired visuals
- Date assigned
- Review dates
- Final completion date

Documents and Results

- Draft RFP
- Similar RFP from the same customer
- SOO/SOW
- Strawman RFP
- Proposal outline

45

45
Draft
proposal
manage-
ment plan

See PROPOSAL
MANAGEMENT PLAN,
Proposal Guide.

Draft proposal management plan

The Proposal Management Plan (PMP) includes the elements to manage proposal development and guide contributors. The content, form, and medium vary by proposal, organization, process, and resources. Formal, document-based proposal management plans are increasingly developed within collaborative web applications and then shared and updated on secure intranet sites.

Keep the PMP current and complete:

- Give the team the *big picture*.
- Keep management and contributors current on daily progress.
- Convey daily tasks, expectations, and quality standards.
- Expose contributors to the same information while reducing misleading rumors.

Identify and summarize information about your organization and the customer organization. Include descriptions of standard proposal preparation processes, roles, and standards. Similarly, describe customer evaluation processes, roles, and standards. The capture plan, prior PMPs, and bid requests from this customer are good sources.

Once the overall framework for the proposal has been developed, the core team can begin to assemble the customer's boilerplate. Do not wait for the RFP to arrive to do this because many items (legal clearance and Certifications and Representations) can and must be pushed through the system. In addition to predictable customer boilerplate, assemble the following items before the RFP arrives:

- Organizational charts of the bidding organizations and the program team
- Flowcharts of relevant processes
- Resumes of named individuals filling key positions
- Descriptions of relevant facilities
- Relevant experience descriptions, quantified performance data, and potential references

Documents and Results

- Draft PMP

46

46
Support
customer
definition of
needs and
require-
ments

Support customer definition of needs and requirements

The proposal manager, the program manager, and technical staff craft a solution that supports customer needs and requirements. Address all customer needs, hot button issues, and requirements.

Explicitly discuss compliance and responsiveness implications of alternate solutions. Evaluators will check compliance, so deviations must be justified and made an explicit part of your capture and proposal strategy.

47

47
Define
detailed
baseline
offering

See ENGAGING PROGRAM
SUPPORT *and* PRICING TO
WIN, *Capture Guide.*

Define detailed baseline offering

Initiate the baseline design as early as possible and work toward an early design freeze. A comprehensive baseline solution includes the technical, management, and pricing solution. Focusing exclusively on the technical solution often leads to an overly elaborate technical solution that is more costly and less competitive.

Seek an early freeze of the solution framework to enable contributors to persuasively describe your solution in storyboards and section drafts, and accurately cost tasks. Shifting solutions lead writers to prepare generic descriptions that are unconvincing, difficult to price, and risky to deliver.

48

48
Receive, review, and comment on draft solicitation

See MODEL DOCUMENT 1, REQUEST FOR RFP MODIFICATION, *Proposal Guide.*

Receive, review, and comment on draft solicitation

Demonstrate your interest and understanding of the customer and their needs by reviewing the draft RFP and making constructive suggestions for improvement. Consider other reasons to respond to the draft RFP:

- Show you are interested in solving the customer's problems.
- Find out who (besides you) helped the customer draft the RFP.
- Establish, in writing, your potential solutions to customer requirements without revealing your solution to competitors.
- Establish your technology as the favored choice or an acceptable option.
- Make sure that you understand the RFP.

Follow these guidelines when responding to draft RFPs:

- Make the core team responsible for analyzing the draft document and formulating the formal response to it.
- Have volume leaders assess the technical, management, and cost elements.

- Draw on specialists in the functional areas—preferably those who will be members of the actual proposal team—for detailed inputs to the draft RFP.
- Avoid requesting general clarification of the draft requirements. Ask specific questions and make specific recommendations.
- Offer revisions or clarifications to the RFP text that the customer can easily insert in a revised RFP.
- Discuss the benefits to the customer for each of the recommended changes to the RFP.

The customer is not just looking for how well you can fulfill particular requirements but how you would refine and improve those requirements to improve the acquisition. Ideally, your response should subtly influence the customer's requirements to favor areas where you are particularly strong and have a competitive advantage.

Documents and Results

- Questions/suggestions for customer

49

49
Update winning price

See PRICING TO WIN, *Capture Guide.*

Remember that the price to win is your best estimate of the customer's desired set of capabilities at a price, not simply a price.

Update winning price

Based on the intelligence collected to date and the draft RFP, the program manager, the proposal manager, and upper management update the price to win. The price to win must 1) be within the winning price window (see figure 26), 2) be capable of winning, and 3) project adequate return on investment for the program.

Pricing-to-win analysis focuses on the trade-offs among this customer's requirements, your capabilities and costs, and competitors' likely strategies and tactics. Developing the price to win with certainty is impossible, but the most effective organizations get close. Customers are either budget limited, capability satisfied, or seek best value. Budget-limited customers seek

the most capability they can afford. Capability-satisfied customers seek the lowest price for the needed capability. Best-value customers have a variable budget and can accept a range of capabilities.

To understand each customer's evolving price/capability trade-off, consider your market knowledge, this customer's budget assumptions, your evolving capabilities, and competitors' evolving capabilities. Focus on competitors' prior strategies, as they tend to recycle them, especially if they were successful.

Documents and Results

- Pricing strategy document

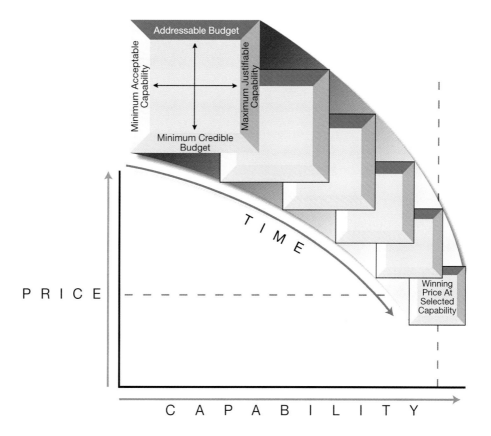

Figure 26. Winning Price Window. *The winning price window, often termed the price to win, narrows over time as customers better understand their needs, budget, and capabilities of potential solutions.*

50   Define cost drivers and update target price in competitive range

Costing in support of the targeted price to win is complex, and if not done well, can sink the project. Normally, the objective is to minimize or balance price against capability; therefore, cost drivers need to be identified early to improve your flexibility in achieving the price to win.

With your cost volume leader and technical personnel, identify those elements that tend to drive costs. Determine if alternate solutions would yield acceptable results at lower cost.

Inform the section writers of the costing rationale. Consider the following costing and pricing relationships and issues:

- Costing must be done top-down and bottom-up.
- Top-down costing can be based on the customer's known budget or parametrics from a prior, similar program.
- Bottom-up costing often leads to over-costing, as safety factors are added at each level by multiple individuals.
- Price targets are influenced by competitors' probable pricing strategies. Approaches that result in a cost below the targeted price are preferable.

See Costing *and* Pricing to Win, *Capture Guide.*

51 Identify proposal team members and assignments

51
Identify proposal team members and assignments

Identify proposal team members, individual assignments, and when they will be involved. Notify team members and their immediate supervisors. Ideally, the proposal manager or volume manager notifies members personally, depending upon the size of the proposal team and the location of members. Proposal manager is a role that might include elements of the capture manager, program manager, proposal support, and author roles on smaller efforts or when resources are limited. Figure 27 shows a notional proposal team structure.

See TEAM SELECTION AND MANAGEMENT, *Proposal Guide*.

```
                    ┌─────────────┐
                    │  Proposal   │
                    │  Manager    │
                    └─────────────┘
   ┌──────────────┐        ┌──────────────┐
   │  Production  │        │   Proposal   │
   │   Support    │        │ Coordinator  │
   └──────────────┘        └──────────────┘
┌────────────┐ ┌────────────┐ ┌────────────┐ ┌────────────┐
│ Technical  │ │ Management │ │    Past    │ │    Cost    │
│  Volume    │ │  Volume    │ │Performance │ │  Volume    │
│  Manager   │ │  Manager   │ │  Volume    │ │  Manager   │
│            │ │            │ │  Manager   │ │            │
└────────────┘ └────────────┘ └────────────┘ └────────────┘
┌─────────────────────────────────────────────────────────┐
│                     Section Authors                      │
└─────────────────────────────────────────────────────────┘
```

Authors or managers might take on production support and coordination tasks.

Small proposals often lack volume managers.

Figure 27. Notional Proposal Team. *Proposal team responsibilities vary by organization and opportunity. On small efforts, multiple roles might be filled by the same individual. The proposal team creates a sales document that is aligned with the capture plan, capture strategy, and your approved solution.*

52 Establish team area and library

52
Establish team area and library

See DAILY TEAM MANAGEMENT, TEAM SELECTION AND MANAGEMENT, *and* VIRTUAL TEAM MANAGEMENT, *Proposal Guide;* ENGAGING PROPOSAL SUPPORT, *Capture Guide*.

Proposal teams need space to work. Physical proposal rooms offer significant collaboration advantages. When managers, writers, editors, and graphic artists work together, an esprit de corps develops, developing a consistent style and tone is easier, coordination is easier, quality improves, and revisions are reduced.

Traditionally, a co-located team has the following facilities:

- Offices or cubicles for the proposal manager and volume leaders
- Work stations with network access for writers, editors, and graphic support for writers, editors, and typists
- Wall space for storyboards, mock-ups, and text
- White board for brainstorming
- At least one meeting room

However, virtual or partially virtual proposal teams are increasingly common and necessary. Virtual teams are more flexible to form, execute, and disband; better talent often becomes available; logistics costs might be reduced; and response time is reduced by eliminating travel time.

If all or substantial portions of your proposal team are virtual, seek virtual equivalents to your usual co-located team management approaches. Consider how team members will meet, obtain library information, collaborate, share drafts, and work with support personnel.

Regardless of the team's operating mode, a proposal library is essential. Include past proposals, lessons learned, reuse material, resumes, past RFPs (ideally from this customer), and competitor information in your proposal library. Keep library information current, promptly posting meeting minutes and current versions of the capture and proposal management plans.

Determine how you will control access and maintain the security of physical and virtual team spaces, equipment, materials, and data. Maintaining data security includes version control. Relying on incorrect or dated information increases your risk, and searching for the correct version or recreating a lost version is expensive.

53

53
Initiate
preparation of
PDWs

See STORYBOARDS AND
MOCKUPS, *Proposal
Guide.*

Proposal tools,
including PDWs, save
time and improve
quality when adapted
and managed to the
effort.

Initiate preparation of PDWs

The proposal manager and the technical
and management proposal leads initiate the
Proposal Development Worksheets (PDWs), or
storyboards, to guide proposal writers. Proposal
management completes as much as possible of
the PDW to clearly define writers' assignments:

- Section title and number
- Author's name
- Page bogey
- Compliance checklist
- Section outline
- Customer issues
- Past performance
- Proposal strategy applicable to the
  author's section

Other guidance may include:

- Technical solution
- Suggested themes
- Features and benefits
- Suggested graphics
- Risk management or mitigation approach

The more guidance proposal management
provides to the authors, the quicker they can
get started on their sections and the greater the
consistency and compatibility they can achieve
across the proposal. One tool to facilitate this is
Shipley's PDW, shown in figure 28.

Documents and Results

- PDWs

Figure 28. Proposal Development Worksheet. *Shipley's storyboarding tool, the PDW,
incorporates best practices in proposal content planning.*

54

54
Prepare
estimating
guidelines

See COSTING, *Capture
Guide.*

Prepare estimating guidelines

Task the cost volume manager to establish
cost estimating guidelines for estimators.
Estimating guidelines enhance the consistency
of estimates, estimating rationale improves,
and contract negotiations will be faster and less
contentious. Summarize estimating guidelines
and assumptions, and insert them in the cost
proposal.

Estimators should work closely with technical
and management contributors so that the task
description and estimate are consistent. Include
the following in your estimating guidelines:

- A definition of the level of WBS that
  proposal costs will be estimated and
  submitted
- An in-house SOW or extended WBS and
  WBS dictionary
- A CLIN/CDRL/WBS/SOW/Functional
  Responsibility matrix

- A list of relevant jobs and historic costs
- A make/buy determination
- Program schedules with dictated
  milestones
- A list of the quality and type of hardware
  required
- Whether cost/schedule reports are
  required (DoD 7000.2 reports)
- A deliverables list
- Relevant financial ground rules, such as
  escalation, facility capitalization, facilities
  and location of work, rates, etc.
- Other relevant baseline data

Documents and Results

- Estimating guidelines

55

55 Create SOW/ WBS/BOE responsi-bility matrix

See COMPLIANCE AND RESPONSIVENESS, *Proposal Guide;* COSTING, *Capture Guide.*

Create a SOW/WBS/BOE responsibility matrix

The cost volume manager creates a BOE (Basis of Estimate) responsibility matrix using the RFP SOW, the WBS, CDRL, and the CLINs, if appropriate, to identify department responsibility by task. In the proposal, all SOW tasks and CLINs must be tied to the WBS.

Prepare a SOW/WBS cross-reference matrix to ensure they are parallel and to help ensure compatibility among the technical, management, and cost volumes. The SOW/ WBS responsibility matrix can also be used as a checklist to ensure all RFP requirements are addressed.

Documents and Results

- Responsibility matrix

56

56 Prepare writers' packages and gather re-use materials; assign cost bogies to BOEs

See KICKOFF MEETINGS *and* PROPOSAL MANAGEMENT PLAN; *Proposal Guide.*

Prepare writers' packages and gather re-use materials; assign cost bogies to BOEs

Proposal managers and volume managers or leads ensure that section writers understand their assignments and the specific tasks they are expected to accomplish. Based on the draft or strawman RFP and your proposal management plan (PMP), create writers' packages that include:

- Author assignments
- Assigned section numbers
- Page bogeys
- Compliance checklists
- Customer issues
- Features and benefits
- Strategy at the proposal, volume, and section levels
- Themes
- Discriminators
- Proposal style sheet

- Proposal development schedule
- Draft executive summary
- WBS and WBS dictionary
- Guidelines on how the bases of estimates will be accomplished
- Team organization chart and roster listing each contributor, organization, and contact information
- Proposal baseline solution
- Writers' standards, guidelines, and sources of support

Give each writer a copy of the PMP or on-line access.

Documents and Results

- Writers' packages

57

57 Draft executive summary

See EXECUTIVE SUMMARY, *Capture Guide* and/or *Proposal Guide.*

Draft executive summary

The capture manager, with assistance from the core capture team, should have mocked-up an executive summary in Step 33 and presented it in the Preliminary Bid Decision Gate review.

In this step, either the capture manager or the proposal manager prepares a full draft of the executive summary. While the capture manager *owns* the executive summary, the assigned author varies depending upon the organization, customer understanding, and relative skills and availability of the capture core team members.

Your draft executive summary might not resemble the final product, but the preparation process helps you refine your proposal strategy, communicates that strategy in-house to all contributors, and models how your proposal will look. Write the executive summary first, edit it repeatedly, and revise it for the last time just before proposal production.

The core team and senior management should review the early draft version of the executive summary. Explain to the reviewers that the draft executive summary reflects your win strategy, themes, overall content, and format of the proposal. Explain further that this summary will be distributed to the full team as guidance for writing.

Documents and Results

- Draft executive summary

58

58
Hold
proposal
kickoff
meeting

See KICKOFF MEETING *and* VIRTUAL TEAM MANAGEMENT, *Proposal Guide*.

Hold proposal kickoff meeting

As a culmination of the core team's preparation, hold the proposal kickoff meeting (see figure 29). Use the draft PMP to explain and get buy-in on the following proposal items:

- Strategy
- Schedule
- Format
- Outline
- Baseline design of the offering

Invite:

- All members of the core team
- Key management, including those who have made and will make critical decisions on this proposal effort
- Key marketers
- Key engineers
- Selected members of the extended proposal team

A key element of a virtual kickoff meeting is the explanation of team and data management procedures and processes. When using web browser-based collaboration tools to document and share information, clearly and thoroughly review access rights, logon procedures, library structure, and notification processes. Promptly post document updates to avoid confusion, lost time, and poor productivity.

Milestones

- Kickoff

Documents and Results

- Proposal kickoff package

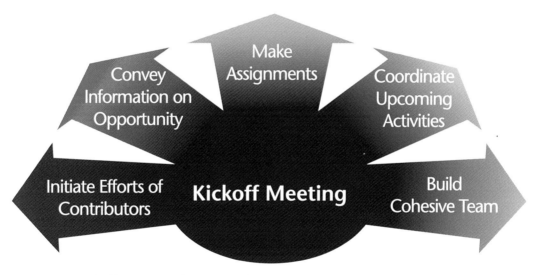

Figure 29. Kickoff Meeting Objectives. *The capture manager and proposal manager use the kickoff meeting to accomplish several objectives. The capture manager discusses the customer, competitors, capture strategy, discriminators, solution, teaming arrangements, and win themes. The proposal manager discusses the preparation process, schedule, roles, quality standards, and how the capture strategy will be implemented in the proposal. A program manager or technical lead might elaborate on the proposed solution. The proposal manager must build a proposal team focused on preparing a clear, compliant, and persuasive proposal given the time and resources available.*

59

59
Complete and review PDWs; prepare mock-ups/ OPPs

See STORYBOARDS
AND MOCKUPS, ORAL
PROPOSALS, *Proposal
Guide*.

Complete and review PDWs; prepare mockups/OPPs

Use Proposal Development Worksheets (PDWs) and mockups to plan, develop, and review new content for proposal sections before writing text. Use them to save time and improve quality.

PDWs have a one-to-one relationship with major sections of the proposal pertaining to a common topic. PDWs list writers' assignments, bid request requirements, strategies, features, benefits, discriminators, preliminary visuals, and content in bullet list form.

The Shipley PDW is a specific type of storyboard. Experienced proposal managers often customize the form, content, and application of storyboards to individual proposal efforts.

The Oral Proposal Planner (OPP) is a variant of a PDW used to help contributors plan an oral proposal. Most proposal managers prepare a PDW linked to an OPP. The structure is aligned.

Part of proposal planning is to decide which proposal sections will be storyboarded. Generally, the newer the requirement, the more you will gain by developing storyboards or PDWs.

Assign PDWs at proposal kickoff. The core team assigns PDWs with guidelines. Writers complete individual PDWs.

Mockups are page-for-page representations of actual pages in the finished proposal. Mockups contain the same elements as the draft; headings, themes, visuals, action captions, and text. Mockups transition writers from the PDW to drafting.

Mockups free writers to work on any portion of a section while maintaining the planned organization. Mockups help prevent over-writing and preserve topic balance.

Writers often are uncomfortable with using PDWs and mockups, thinking that they should just begin drafting text. Train writers to use PDWs and mockups. Used correctly, PDWs and mockups reduce iterations and revisions, save time, and improve proposal quality.

Documents and Results

- PDWs and mockups/OPPs (Oral Proposal Planners)

60

60
Hold peer review and finalize materials for Pink Team

See COLOR TEAM
REVIEWS, *Capture
Guide*.

Hold peer review and finalize materials for Pink Team

Determine what you will review at your Pink Team. Some proposal managers schedule more than one Pink Team review. In general, review only PDWs and mockups at the first Pink Team review; review drafts in subsequent Pink Team reviews after receiving the final RFP.

Peer reviews are scheduled before color team reviews, especially the Pink Team review. Ask contributors to review and make constructive recommendations for improvements to materials prepared by their peers. Implement constructive suggestions and prepare the materials for the Pink Team review.

Prepare an ordered, comprehensive package for Pink Team reviewers:

- Volume leaders assemble PDWs and mockup in order.
- Volume leaders add volume summaries and introductions before the PDWs.
- The proposal manager inserts the current version of the executive summary.
- The proposal manager organizes the materials, facility, and briefing materials according to the instructions of the Pink Team review facilitator.

Adapt review materials, instructions, and tools to the review, whether co-located, virtual, or blended.

61

61

Hold Pink Team review, including cost volume and initial bottom-up cost estimate

Hold Pink Team review, including cost volume and initial bottom-up cost estimate

Hold a Pink Team review to ensure:

- Compliance with the customer's requirements
- Implementation of agreed-upon strategy
- Consistency of volumes

Pink Team reviews are an invaluable project control—a means of solving problems before they occur. A high-level Pink Team review assesses how well the proposal strategy is implemented in the PDWs and mockups.

A major issue with color team reviews, including the Pink Team review, is securing knowledgeable, skilled, experienced, and constructive reviewers. Skilled reviewers are invariably overscheduled, so set a date in the proposal schedule well in advance of the review date to identify, invite, and confirm reviewers' participation.

Post PDWs and mockups on the war room walls or panels or on an intranet site when the Pink Team review is virtual. These pages reveal the proposal's structure, compliance, responsiveness, strategy, and competitive focus. The Pink Team reviews the strawman draft, too, but mainly critiques the draft proposal for:

- Compliance
- Strategy
- Visuals
- Themes
- Space allocation
- Organizational compliance with the proposal outline
- Overall cohesiveness

See Color Team Reviews, *Capture Guide.*

Select high-level managers representing technical, management, cost, contractual, and legal issues. Overlap key Pink Team and Red Team reviewers. This continuity often minimizes radical differences in their recommendations.

Pink Team recommendations are preliminary until you receive the final RFP. However, Pink Team recommendations help the proposal manager and the core team solve problems early in the process.

Review all portions of the proposal. Ask the cost volume manager to create a Contract Line Item (CLIN) WBS matrix that includes:

- Description and summary of each item
- How each item relates to the WBS
- The department responsible for addressing each item

Ask the Pink Team to check the compliance and responsiveness of this matrix. Figure 30 shows the expected inputs and outputs associated with an effective Pink Team review.

Milestones

- Pink Team

Documents and Results

- Pink Team report and recommendations

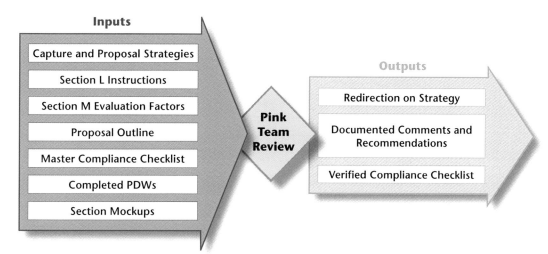

Figure 30. Pink Team Inputs and Outputs. *The Pink Team determines whether the proposal is on track, preferably before authors spend time writing text. A good Pink Team prevents authors from writing with improper emphasis or even about the wrong topics.*

62

62 Update PDWs and mock-ups/ OPPs in response to Pink Team

See ORAL PROPOSALS, *and* STORYBOARDS AND MOCKUPS, *Proposal Guide.*

Update PDWs and mockups/OPPs in response to Pink Team

The Pink Team debriefs the core proposal team. The core team (with section leaders and writers where necessary) reviews Pink Team recommendations, decides which recommendations are valid, revises the proposal strategy, and tasks volume managers to direct revisions to the PDWs and mockups.

The objective is to improve:

- Alignment with the proposal strategy
- Alignment among sections
- Clarity and specificity
- Links to experience and performance examples

63

63 Begin early draft/ presentation development (if required to meet goals)

See STORYBOARDS AND MOCKUPS, *Proposal Guide.*

Begin early draft/presentation development (if required to meet goals)

If time permits, this is a must-win proposal, and you are reasonably confident that the strawman or draft RFP will not change drastically, ask section writers to draft strawman text and visuals. Creating text now makes their tasks easier when the actual RFP arrives but only if there are minimal changes. Relatively few organizations have the time or resources to draft significant portions of the text before the final bid request is released.

However, drafting the executive summary as a model for the proposal team is a good practice. Make the executive summary a model showing the proposal page design.

At this early stage, focus on writing summaries, theme statements, introductions, and action captions. Limit body text to lists of topics or points that you plan to discuss in the proposal or presentation.

Identify the programs that you will cite as relevant past performance. Relevant programs involve common or similar key personnel, services, products, issues, customers, schedules, contract values, team members, and management processes.

64

64 Receive and analyze customer solicitation

See COMPLIANCE AND RESPONSIVENESS, OUTLINING, *Proposal Guide.*

Receive and analyze customer solicitation

The proposal core team, consisting of the proposal manager, volume leads, and perhaps the proposal coordinator, analyzes the bid request. Experts from sales, marketing, and engineering might also assist.

Despite your best intelligence, bid request requirements and technical specifications often change. Generally, a committee writes the RFP, so often an RFP is inconsistent in parts. This is especially true when the RFP has not been issued in draft for industry review.

The proposal manager should read the RFP carefully (several times) to understand the requirements and determine how to respond. The proposal manager should read the RFP with the core team and verify that they share the same interpretation.

Read the RFP several times. Skim the RFP to get a feel for the entire document. Gain an overall understanding of the RFP and procurement. If possible, let an entire day pass before your next, detailed review.

Re-read the RFP and take extensive notes. Identify areas where the RFP is vague, confusing, or inconsistent. Discuss these parts with your core team. Make notes in the margin indicating the connections and cross-references between requirements throughout the RFP.

Develop compliance checklists for all areas in the RFP. Look for these common types of requirements:

- Customer needs/problems
- Technical performance or operational specifications
- Deliverables, including CDRLs
- Schedule
- Proposal requirements/format/ organization
- Evaluation criteria

The focus at this step is to understand, analyze, and summarize these requirements at the upcoming Bid Validation Decision Gate review. If management decides to proceed with a bid, you will refine this compliance checklist and integrate the requirements within the annotated proposal outline.

65

65
Prepare final bid/no-bid recommen- dation

See DECISION GATE REVIEWS, *Capture Guide.*

Prepare final bid/no-bid recommendation

Identify exactly what senior managers expect to be presented at a Bid Validation Decision Gate review and prepare to present those materials. The primary gate review decision is whether the opportunity is still worth pursuing and to verify that "show stoppers" have been addressed.

The capture core team, comprising the individuals in the capture, program, and proposal manager roles, prepare the final bid/ no-bid recommendation. End the pursuit of opportunities that you are unlikely to win, saving half or more of the business development costs associated with the opportunity.

66

66
Review and validate the bid decision

See DECISION GATE REVIEWS, *Capture Guide.*

Review and validate the bid decision

The customer's issuance of the final bid request precipitates the Bid Validation Decision Gate review. Revisit your preliminary bid decision, considering the following questions:

- Does the final RFP reflect your input to the draft RFP?
- Did the customer incorporate many or a few of your recommendations?
- Were the most significant changes suggested by you or competitors?
- If the RFP contains significant new language and requirements, what was the source?

Make the final bid validation decision within 1 day of receiving the RFP.

Milestones

- Bid validation decision

Documents and Results

- Updated bid/no-bid recommendation

Proposal Development should begin promptly after receiving the RFP and a positive bid validation decision. Carefully plan proposal preparation tasks, make clear individual task assignments, set firm milestone and inch-stone completion dates, and monitor progress daily. Reduce preparation time by working in parallel.

Resist the urge to hold an immediate proposal team kickoff meeting until you can make clear contributor assignments. Instead, review your process, finalize your plan and schedule, and conduct an effective kickoff meeting. Figure 31 shows recommended steps for this phase.

See PROCESS, *Capture Guide.*

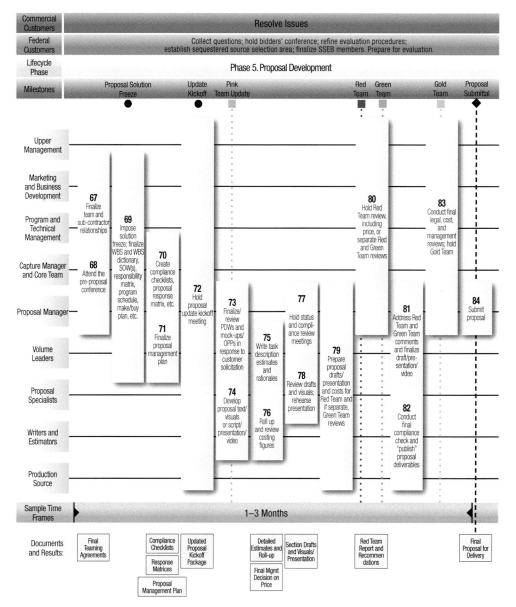

Figure 31. Phase 5: Proposal Development. *Proposal development is the phase where you prepare a persuasive sales document or presentation. The initiating decision gate is the Bid Validation Gate review; the concluding decision gate is the Proposal Submittal Decision Gate review.*

67

67
Finalize team
and sub-
contractor
relationships

See TEAMING, *Capture
Guide.*

Finalize team and subcontractor relationships

If intending to team or subcontract with another organization, most terms have been discussed. Finalize those arrangements consistent with changes in the RFP. Key elements include:

- Finalize legal arrangements, which often require reviews and signatures of senior managers and attorneys.
- Finalize teaming-subcontracting arrangements, work share, and proposal preparation support roles and responsibilities.
- Determine the delivery team structure, key personnel, and management processes needed to prepare the management volume (e.g., organizational charts, management charts, descriptions of duties to be performed by each organization, etc.).

- Verify teaming partner and subcontractors' past performance data and references are accurate.

Ideally, you have negotiated an exclusive relationship with subcontractors. If not, share information carefully. Balance your need to protect business confidential information with subcontractors' need to know to contribute to a winning solution and proposal.

Documents and Results

- Final teaming agreements

68

68
Attend the
pre-proposal
conference

Attend the pre-proposal conference

Often customers schedule a pre-proposal conference after issuing an RFP inviting all organizations who have responded to the draft RFP, registered with the customer expressing their interest, or requested copies of the RFP.

The customer generally gives a short presentation on the program, including clarification of any problem areas that have come up since the RFP was issued. Bidders are then allowed to ask questions about the RFP or the program. Some government agencies record these conferences and distribute copies upon request.

Take careful notes, including the question, questioner, response, and responder. Observe and record the reactions of others at the conference. Customer representatives, such as the contracting officer, the contracting officer's technical representative, and the program manager, are influential participants who want to meet the bidders and ensure that everyone understands the requirements, needs, and evaluation criteria.

Consider attendance mandatory. Some customers require bidders to attend to be eligible to bid. Others interpret non-attendance as non-interest. Either way, the intelligence that you gain reduces your bidding risk and is often revealing about competitors.

Customers often limit attendees. If limited to two participants, start with the capture manager and program manager. Increase attendees by having key teammates, subcontractor representatives, and consultants attend.

Carefully consider what questions to ask, how to ask a question, and what your question might reveal to the customer and competitors. Anything the customer and participants discuss during the pre-proposal conference does not carry the force of law. To change the RFP, the customer must issue a formal, written change addendum.

Every question reveals something about the questioner. One aspect of strategy should be to scrutinize the competitors' questions. What they ask might reveal their uncertainties and weaknesses. Consider whether the customer's responses helped your competitor. Your questions are as revealing to competitors as their questions are to you.

Some questions are purely administrative: "Does the Privacy Act apply to this procurement?" It hardly matters who asks this sort of question, but it can be embarrassing. For example, the customer's reply may be, "Read the RFP."

Other questions are eye-openers: "Would wing-mounted Fantastic Gizmos be an acceptable approach to the attenuation problems noted under Paragraph 8.3c of the Design Requirements?" This question potentially reveals much about the organization asking the question. If truly considering using a wing-mounted Fantastic Gizmo, would an organization ask a question revealing so much to its competitors?

Use the pre-proposal conference to learn more about the procurement. Do not reveal your technical or management approach. Ideally, you have resolved your questions before the RFP was issued. If you go to the conference with substantial management and technical questions, you reveal much to competitors and might prompt the customer to question your understanding and competence.

Obtain the contractor sign-in log before leaving, if possible. Identify competitors, potential teaming partners, and potential teaming combinations.

A potential tactic is to ask intelligent technical questions that suggest you are pursuing a technical approach that will be less attractive or practical than your competitors' likely approaches. While this type of misdirection strategy might lull competitors into a false sense of security, do not appear foolish to the customer or competitors. Consider whether competitors are employing a similar strategy.

69

69
Impose solution freeze; finalize WBS and WBS dictionary, SOW(s), responsibility matrix, program schedule, make/buy plan, etc.

See COMPLIANCE AND RESPONSIVENESS, *Proposal Guide;* COSTING, *and* PRICING TO WIN; *Capture Guide.*

Impose solution freeze; finalize WBS and WBS dictionary, SOW(s), responsibility matrix, program schedule, make/buy plan, etc.

Meeting the customer's deadline is challenging, even when the proposal machinery runs smoothly. Repeated changes in your solution, strategy, teaming partners, proposal organization, proposal preparation schedule, and work-share often result in a mediocre proposal that was frustrating to prepare.

The capture core team should present the solution at the Bid Validation Decision Gate review. Shortly after the positive bid validation decision, the core capture and proposal teams should implement recommended refinements and freeze the solution so you can focus on preparing a clear, concise, and persuasive proposal. Freeze the solution with the firm support of your senior management champion for this pursuit.

A common mistake is to permit repeated improvements in the solution, whether real or imagined. You are more likely to win by submitting a superior proposal with an adequate solution than a superior solution in a poor proposal.

Set a design-freeze date, obtain the endorsement of your program champion, enter it on the proposal preparation schedule, and emphasize it at the proposal kickoff meeting and subsequent daily stand-up meetings.

If the RFP includes a WBS, extend it into a contractor WBS. A contractor WBS aligns with your cost accounting system and assigns task responsibility to organizations and departments.

Develop a WBS dictionary that defines each task and the boundaries between tasks. Fuzzy boundaries lead to confusion, double pricing, or under pricing. The WBS dictionary clarifies program tasks for estimators and the customer. It also helps team members track and report WBS item costs during program development.

Some RFPs require that you submit a WBS dictionary. Prepare the WBS and WBS dictionary at the level of detail needed to accurately estimate your costs, but propose at the level of detail that you are willing to report when executing the program. The more detailed your proposed WBS, the greater your program management cost.

If the RFP requires an Integrated Master Plan, Integrated Master Schedule, or Performance Work Statements, align the WBS with these requirements.

Identify, integrate, and manage these tasks by preparing a proposal responsibility matrix. A proposal responsibility matrix links proposal sections, RFP sections and requirements, responsible author, page limits or guidelines, WBS and SOW items, Contract Line Items (CLINs), and Contract Data Requirements.

Milestones

- Proposal solution freeze

70

70
Create
compliance
checklists,
proposal
response
matrix, etc.

See COMPLIANCE
AND RESPONSIVENESS,
Proposal Guide.

Create compliance checklists, proposal response matrix, etc.

Carefully read RFP sections and develop a compliance checklist (see figure 32). Compliance checklists help ensure complete responsiveness by identifying each requirement and relating each requirement to the appropriate RFP paragraph. They are the basis for the proposal outline and response matrix.

1. Follow the order of topics and paragraphs in the bid request. Within paragraphs, follow the order of sentences.

2. List each requirement as a separate checklist item. If a sentence or paragraph contains two or more requirements, then list each requirement as a separate item.

3. Use the customer's words and phrases in the checklist. Do NOT paraphrase. Use the customer's language.

4. Begin each item with the action verb used in the bid request, such as *identify, list, discuss, show, indicate, demonstrate,* and *describe*. These verbs tell the proposal writer what the customer wants to see in the proposal.

5. Use the compliance checklist as a guide to write each section. Base your section outline on the checklist, and follow the order of topics exactly as it appears in the checklist.

6. Periodically check to see that every requirement has been met.

Figure 32. Building a Compliance Checklist. *Compliance checklists are time-consuming to develop. Create them in three steps: 1) Capture all requirements verbatim, no matter how insignificant, without worrying about duplications or contradictions, 2) Divide compound requirements into single requirements, 3) Simplify them into straightforward technical statements or action verb phrases, organize them conveniently, eliminate duplication, and resolve contradictions (with the customer when possible).*

The proposal outline is driven by a combination of the proposal instructions and evaluation criteria, which are largely independent of the checklist. The checklist is linear, listing each requirement. The outline and requirements checklist must be integrated; every requirement must be assigned to one, and ideally only one, place within the proposal outline.

Volume leaders use compliance checklists to construct response matrices (for submission with the proposal) to help reviewers locate responses and determine whether the proposal is compliant.

Place the proposal response matrix in the contents portion of your proposal. In addition, consider placing major section-specific response matrices at the beginning or ending of major sections. Those at the beginning are convenient; those at the ending reinforce your compliance while summarizing your response.

If compliance checklists based on the draft RFP were completed, update them based on the final RFP (see figure 33). If compliance checklists were not developed, create them for the final RFP.

Documents and Results

- Compliance checklists
- Response matrices

Figure 33. Using Compliance Checklists. *Build a compliance checklist from the RFP. Capture every requirement. Then use it during proposal planning, writing, and reviewing to verify that section authors properly address assigned requirements. Also use it to develop a response matrix or locator to include in the proposal for the convenience of evaluators.*

71

71
Finalize
proposal
management
plan

Finalize proposal management plan

All information relevant to planning, managing, and producing the proposal goes into the PMP. Keep the PMP current to reduce confusion and the need for revisions.

While the PMP is referred to as if it were a single document, it typically consists of multiple documents that are often posted on a protected, intra-company web site. When contributors and managers are in multiple locations and working on multiple projects, a web-accessible solution is preferable to a single planning document. Include the following information when updating the PMP:

See PROPOSAL
MANAGEMENT PLAN *and*
SCHEDULING, *Proposal
Guide.*

- Additional background data on the program, customer, and competition gathered since the preliminary plan was drafted
- Adjusted dates, times, resources, and activities on the schedule
- Specific dates for the various project deadlines; use Gantt charts to show the project's overall chronology and overlapping functions
- Brief discussions of major milestones and key events, including kickoff meeting, status, and proposal reviews
- Proposal strategy
- Compliance checklists
- Proposal outline
- Individual writing assignments, page limitations, and deadlines
- Proposal style sheet, including customer and in-house requirements
- Links or references to supporting documents and plans. Some customer-mandated plans will be required at proposal submittal or by a specified date. Other plans are internal, such as a Negotiation Plan

Develop your proposal schedule by tailoring the 96-step process to your process, proposal metrics, and the type/scope of proposal. Develop the schedule in the following order:

1. Insert the major milestones:
   - Bid decision
   - Strawman or draft RFP availability date
   - Pink Team review of the strawman proposal
   - Final RFP release date
   - Kickoff meeting
   - Design freeze date
   - Pink Team review
   - Red Team review
   - Final internal review/approval process
   - Required proposal submission date

2. Schedule backwards from the customer's proposal due date to the RFP release date.
3. Consider how vendors or team members and consultants will interact with the schedule:
   - When do writers and consultants need to be available?
   - What things must be ready for them and when?
4. Develop the subtasks or inch-stone activities for each major milestone and show how they integrate with the schedule.
5. Consider how Bid and Proposal (B&P) costs can be minimized through effective scheduling:
   - Avoid scheduling color team reviews on Mondays or Tuesdays if the people preparing the review materials will require double or triple hourly wages because they worked over the weekend.
   - Assign section writers when you can make clear assignments with clear preparation guidelines: Prepare the RFP outline, schedule, compliance checklists, writing assignments, page bogeys, strategy, and WBS before the kickoff meeting.
   - Start with the proposal due date and work backwards with all detailed tasks.
6. Schedule weekdays. Use weekends as catch-up days, not part of the normal schedule. When you have a large proposal team and teaming partners, discuss whether to include extensive strategy discussions in the proposal project plan. Consider several facets:
   - Company policy
   - Sensitivity of the procurement
   - Proprietary nature of the approach
   - Relationship with team members
   - Relationship with vendors
   - The existence of a secure team area

Balance the *need to know* against the need to protect proprietary information. The more information shared with proposal contributors beyond their actual writing assignments, the more they feel a part of the *big picture* and part of the team. This also avoids the trap of mushroom management that leads to an assembly-line mentality where contributors do not understand their roles in the overall effort.

Documents and Results

- PMP

72

72
Hold
proposal
update kickoff
meeting

Hold proposal update kickoff meeting

Kickoff meetings should be motivational, informative, and directive. The proposal manager should run the kickoff meeting, with support from the capture and program managers.

Plan the meeting carefully, invite contributors and their managers, and prepare custom writers' packages for contributors. Set the agenda, stick to your agenda, and conduct the meeting professionally. Contributors assume that you will manage the proposal like you manage the kickoff meeting.

Invite your senior management champion to kick off the meeting. Ask them to summarize management's vision, objectives, justification, and support for bidding and winning this program.

Hold a proposal update kickoff meeting to announce, confirm, and coordinate changes in the following items:

- Proposal strategy and win themes
- Proposal outline
- Page allocations
- Program organization, resumes, and Integrated Product and Process Teams (IPPT)
- Costing strategy and estimating guidelines
- Task descriptions and BOE procedures
- Writer assignments
- Proposal development schedule milestones

See KICKOFF MEETINGS and VIRTUAL TEAM MANAGEMENT, *Proposal Guide.*

- Proposal operations
- Teammate or vendor assignments
- File transfers, graphics, and data flow to production
- Security controls
- Editing, proofreading, and publication operations
- Technical or management solutions
- Cost as an Independent Variable (CAIV) approach
- Program selections for Past Performance
- Re-use or boilerplate material
- Coordination among writers/volume managers and teammates

Some proposals require multiple kickoff meetings and incorporate virtual meeting elements. For example, you might schedule a separate or supplemental kickoff meeting with teaming partners, subcontractors, or estimators. Some or all participants might have to attend virtually, which requires specific accommodations.

Milestones

- Update kickoff

Documents and Results

- Updated proposal kickoff package

73

73
Finalize/review
PDWs and
mock-ups/
OPPs in
response to
customer
solicitation

Finalize/review PDWs and mockups/OPPs in response to customer solicitation

Having been given an updated proposal outline and strategy, writers review and update their PDWs. When several PDWs link to common topics, ask volume managers to facilitate brainstorming sessions to rapidly stimulate new and congruent ideas.

Then writers update their PDWs, develop stage two mockups, and review both with peers. Stage two mockups include headings, theme statements, summaries, introductory bullet-lists of key points, notations indicating a graphic

See STORYBOARDS AND MOCKUPS, *Proposal Guide.*

(table, chart, drawing, photo), and the action caption. Draft the text after the PDW and mockup are approved by the volume manager.

Some proposal managers expand this review into a Pink Team Update review.

Milestones

- Pink Team Update

74

74
Develop
proposal text/
visuals
or script/
presentation
video

See ACTION CAPTIONS,
CUSTOMER FOCUS,
GRAPHICS, ORGANIZATION,
PHOTOGRAPHS, *and*
THEME STATEMENTS,
Proposal Guide.

Develop proposal text/visuals or script/presentation/video

Proposal evaluators repeatedly say that they are drawn to the visual elements of a proposal first; then they read the text if needed to answer questions and score the response.

Senior decision makers and key influencers have little time to review proposals, so they focus on the visual elements and opening bursts of text.

Proposal writers that focus on the visual elements and key text messages first cut writing time, reduce the number of revisions, and prepare shorter sections. If you have answered the question in the visual and action caption, you do not have to repeat your answer in body text.

Have writers create at least one primary visual for each proposal section. If a section is lengthy and has several major subsections, each subsection should have a key visual.

The purpose of the primary section visual should be to convey the section's central theme or selling point. Essentially, the primary section visual states the section theme statement in visual form.

Ask writers the following questions to help them think about presenting major ideas visually:

- What is the overall point of this section? What exactly is this selling?

- What are the central technical ideas? What data will support these ideas?

- Which medium (words or visuals) will best sell ideas to the customer? How can this presentation best convey the key selling points?

- What visual concept best expresses the central message? Is this showing a relationship (as in a chart), a process (flow or tree diagram), relative size (pie chart), precise data (table), realistic depiction of an object (photograph), representation of internal structure (schematic or cut-away diagram), or sequence of events over time (Gantt chart)?

- What level of generality or specificity does this section address? Is it presenting an overview discussion or a finely detailed technical subsection? In other words, what level of generality or specificity should the visuals depict?

- Is this visual describing complex processes or complicated relationships? Will readers be able to grasp a visual representation better and faster than they could grasp the subject if it were described verbally?

- What kinds of visuals will be most effective for the evaluators who will be scoring this section? What kind of visual would compel the evaluators to score this section higher? What would be compelling?

Conceiving a graphic and creating the graphic are different skills. Ask a graphic specialist to brainstorm graphic concepts with writers. Alternatively, ask writers to draft a complete action caption for each graphic and then discuss their concept with the graphic specialist. Often the graphic specialist will suggest a more effective graphic.

75

75
Write task
description
estimates
and rationales

See COSTING, *Capture
Guide.*

Write task description estimates and rationales

Improve the alignment between technical and management proposal sections and the cost volume by having writers prepare time and material estimates and rationales for their assigned tasks. Then cost analysts can add overhead rates, develop cost estimates, and aggregate costs.

Using cost estimating sheets, section writers and cost analysts write detailed descriptions of the work to be performed, the estimate, and the rationale behind the estimate. Rationale includes actual cost history or comparisons to other projects.

Similarly for service contracts, prepare accurate descriptions of the experience, education, and skill levels within each labor category. Specify their relative level within a labor category.

Consider the percentage of their time devoted to this contract and other contracts. Pricers need this information to accurately price each task.

Differentiate whether a person is a manager or task lead. Evaluators tend to think managers only manage, while task leads also complete tasks. Consider acceptable spans of control given the complexity of the task.

If pricing an ongoing service, consider the current pay grades and rates, and your approach to the incumbent work force. Many bid requests limit your options.

Documents and Results

- Detailed estimates and roll-up

76

76
Roll up and review costing figures

See Costing *and* Pricing to Win, *Capture Guide.*

Roll-up and review costing figures

Each organization's costing process is based on their cost estimating software, so the exact approach varies. The cost volume or estimating manager reviews individual estimates for credibility, rationale, compliance, and completeness. They roll-up costs for program components, and sanity check these totals against prior similar programs. They note unusual differences, probe for an explanation, and correct assumptions or errors.

Small changes in the WBS often force complete re-costing, so freeze the WBS early.

If the project is not re-costed after every change in the WBS:

- Costs are wrong
- Pricing is wrong
- Credibility is lost
- Chances of winning drop

Documents and Results

- Final management decision on price

77

77
Hold status and compliance review meetings

See Daily Team Management, and Virtual Team Management, *Proposal Guide.*

Hold status and compliance review meetings

Conduct status and compliance meetings every morning for a major undertaking or weekly for smaller projects. Determine who needs to attend based on the size and complexity of the project and the relative experience of team members.

Keep daily status meetings short. Schedule small, specific side meetings to solve problems.

Focus primarily on near-term or inch-stone tasks but within the broad context of major milestones. Contributors are more productive when repeatedly focused on what must be completed today rather than next month.

Managing a virtual proposal team or a team with virtual contributors presents unique challenges. Adapt your management approach when you have virtual contributors.

The status meeting should accomplish these objectives:

- Monitor each volume, section, and subsection
- Keep team members informed of the project's status
- Discover problems early before they grow
- Check compliance with organization and customer requirements

78

78
Review drafts and visuals; rehearse presentation

See Oral Proposals, Persuasion, and Presentations to Customers; *Capture Guide.*

Review drafts and visuals; rehearse presentation

Review progress on section drafts to help ensure consistency with other sections, responsiveness, strategy implementation effectiveness, clear communication, and persuasive messages.

Make comments constructive, clear, and positive. Assign people to review drafts and visuals. Reviewers may be section leaders on major projects or volume leaders on medium to small projects.

Assign review dates in the project plan. Review dates—seemingly flexible and relatively unimportant—are crucial to keeping the project on schedule. If one small subsection is incomplete or missing, the entire section is defective.

The objective of the review is to control the section's focus, accuracy, strategy, and selling features. Review and revise each unit until your message comes through according to plan. Edit and proofread sections only after this review.

When preparing a proposal presentation, place equal emphasis on the visual/content elements and the presentation elements. A common mistake is to spend 90 percent on the content and 10 percent on the presentation.

Orchestrate the presentation, train and coach presenters, and rehearse repeatedly in an environment that simulates the anticipated presentation environment. Anticipate difficult questions, prepare responses, and rehearse responders.

Documents and Results

- Section drafts and visuals/presentation

79 — Prepare proposal drafts/presentation and costs for Red Team and, if separate, Green Team reviews

The Red Team should review a complete draft proposal beginning with the executive summary, all volumes including cost, and other items required at submittal. The Green Team should review the near-final pricing. Expect to brief the reviewers and have opportunity-specific, capture, and proposal planning materials available. When consultants and subcontractors are involved, management is often reluctant to share pricing information. Cost reviewers might need to be entirely different from the reviewers of other volumes.

When volume leaders and section writers are satisfied with section drafts, they submit them to editors for stylistic improvement and consistency. After approving the revised and edited sections, the volume leaders submit the drafts to publications so the copy can be produced for final reviews.

All proposal contributors must write, but they won't all write the same way. A proposal manager, volume leader, or section leader must manage (coach) the writers and, thereby, manage their writing.

Based on the results of the cost review, the section writers and cost analysts revise their cost and task descriptions. The cost volume manager assembles the cost volume using the mockup, the RFP requirements, and all the material developed for the cost volume (i.e., WBS, cost summaries, CDRL matrix, SOW/WBS responsibility matrix, etc.).

Most contributors think that they are acceptable writers, but they are uncomfortable with the writing process and having their writing critiqued. Contributors tend to balk at writing, write too little, or over-write:

- When they fail to start or underwrite, they prompt schedule slippages and last-minute recovery actions.
- When they over-write, they often include non-relevant or redundant material and create more work for editors, proposal managers, and reviewers.

Identify, isolate, and remedy typical writers' problems. Figure 34 contains several examples. The review and revision process is iterative. Encourage writers to use PDWs and mockups to reduce revision cycles, save time, and reduce preparation costs. Monitor writers' progress daily.

POTENTIAL PROBLEM	POSSIBLE SOLUTION
Some writers can't get started. Perhaps they are not sure what they are going to say, don't clearly understand the task, or the task is so overwhelming that they can't decide where and how to begin.	Brainstorm in a group or individually. Either way, the point is to get as many ideas or concepts written as quickly as possible. Write as fast as possible. Do not judge, edit, or organize.
Some writers lose sight of their goals because they forget the purpose of their writing (or were never given a purpose to begin with). They may write a great deal, but it is an unfocused "dump."	Give writers clear, precise strategies and theme statements to help them focus their sections. Discuss with them how their sections fit into the proposal. Writers need a focused perspective.
Some writers have trouble organizing their thoughts, often because they can't decide what is of primary importance and what is secondary.	Use clustering or outlining techniques to assist writers in prioritizing and organizing their material. Clustering—literally drawing circles connected by lines—works especially well with visually oriented people. The more traditional method of outlining works well with people who feel comfortable with structure and words.
Some writers know what they want to say but can't put the right words on paper to express it. They can explain their material orally but falter when left alone to write.	Use rehearsing techniques to get writers talking about their sections and orally practicing idea formation, organization, and expression. Without actually writing, writers can try out organizational patterns, words, and sentences, answering the manager's questions along the way until the best organizational and language approaches are found. Stop the writer often to jot down a summary of what has been said so far or even record the session, giving the tape to the writer at session's end.
Some writers insert existing material, feeling that it was already written, reviewed, accepted, and submitted before. Why write new material?	Use reuse material to stimulate thinking and identify potentially, relevant points. Insist that each requirement be answered succinctly, then adapt the boilerplate to support the summary answer. Emphasize the four-box organization, including only directly relevant material.

Figure 34. Preparing Proposal Drafts for Red Team. *A successful proposal manager knows his/her team, is able to anticipate problems, and is able to craft appropriate solutions—hopefully before the problem occurs.*

80

80
Hold Red
Team review,
including
price, or
separate Red
and Green
Team reviews

See Color Team Reviews, *Capture Guide.*

Hold Red Team review, including price, or separate Red and Green Team reviews

A Red Team is an in-house proposal review team that reads and evaluates the draft proposal from the customer's perspective. A Green Team is an in-house cost review team that compares your pricing against your technical, management, and other non-price solution components to confirm everything is included in the estimate.

The Red Team conducts a mock evaluation of the proposal, applying the same scoring methods evaluators would use. By nurturing customer relations, gathering good intelligence, and carefully analyzing RFP Section M, you can often determine the scoring system evaluators will employ. The Red Team also checks inter-volume compatibility.

For example, the proposal claims the following:

- The Technical Volume defines Task A.
- The Management Volume states that Task A will require 6,000 person-hours.
- The Cost Volume states that Task A at 6,000 person-hours will cost $1.5 million.

The Red Team verifies the validity of each volume and related claims among the volumes. Is Task A properly defined? Will it require 6,000 person-hours? Is $1.5 million for Task A reasonable and realistic? The proposal is not credible when facts and messages conflict. Evaluators invariably cross-check volumes and either reduce your score or challenge your claims during contract negotiations.

After reviewing and scoring the proposal, the Red Team typically debriefs the proposal team, offering suggestions for improvements to the overall proposal and specific proposal sections.

The Red Team must be intimately familiar with the RFP and all pre-RFP intelligence. While the capture or proposal manager often briefs the Red Team on the strategy and solution, these elements should be obvious in the proposal. Minimize conflicting recommendations by overlapping color team reviewers, if possible.

The proposal manager should make the following items available to Red Team reviewers:

- Capture and proposal management plans
- RFP documents and analysis, including the outline and response matrix (should be in the proposal)
- List of discriminators
- Bidder comparison charts
- Notes on procurement intelligence

The Red Team leader should:

- Ensure that all members are familiar with RFP evaluation requirements
- Develop an evaluation scheme, instructions, schedule, assignments, rating system, and approach to consolidate recommendations

The Red Team review must be positive, productive, and efficient. The primary goal is to improve the proposal's win probability; the secondary goal is to ensure compliance, responsiveness, and enhance the skills of contributors for future proposals.

At a high level, the Red Team review addresses the following questions:

- What is the overall effect of the proposal? Does it sell? Does it represent you in the best possible manner?
- Is the proposal customer focused? Does it clearly and consistently project the proposal strategy?
- Are theme statements and headlines used effectively?
- How responsive is the proposal to all RFP and administrative requirements?
- Are discriminators used to highlight our strengths and competitors' weaknesses, mitigate our weaknesses, and neutralize competitors' strengths?
- Are features linked to benefits, preferably with the benefits stated first?
- Is the proposal organization consistent with what the customer requires?
- Are emphatic devices (headings, lists, white space) used effectively?
- Are visual aids (graphics) used effectively?
- Is the writing style crisp and clear? Are verbs active rather than passive?
- Is the proposal attractively packaged (cover letter, binding, reproduction)?

Figure 35 summarizes the inputs and outputs associated with an effective Red Team review.

Milestones

- Red Team
- Green Team

Documents and Results

- Red Team report and recommendations
- Green Team report and recommendations

Figure 35. Red Team Inputs and Outputs. *The Red Team offers the last chance to improve a proposal before delivery. Small revisions are usually made by a core management group, but bigger problems may require redrafting entire sections. Changes of that magnitude should be caught at Pink Team and corrected in the pre-Red Team draft.*

81

81
Address Red Team and Green Team comments and finalize draft/pre-sentation/video

See ORGANIZATION *and* REVIEWS, *Proposal Guide; and* COLOR TEAM REVIEWS, *Capture Guide.*

Address Red Team and Green Team comments and finalize draft/presentation/video

After the Red Team and Green Team reviews, decide what recommendations will be accepted, specify the change, and determine who will make the proposal revision. This decision depends on the amount and type of revision the teams specify.

Asking the primary authors to make revisions is often resisted by the authors, difficult to manage, and creates chaos. Instead, assign specialists to horizontal and vertical revision teams.

Each review team moves through the volumes horizontally (themes and visuals) or vertically (text) making similar corrections to particular aspects of the proposal.

The horizontal review team for themes reworks theme statements, ignoring the visuals and the text. This team asks:
- Do themes sell by linking features to benefits?
- Do selected themes identify you and the customer?
- Are themes as specific as the occasion will allow?

The horizontal review team for visuals reworks the visuals and action captions, ignoring the themes and the text. This team asks:
- Are the visuals complete?
- Can they stand alone?
- Are they cluttered?

- Would a multi-frame visual work better?
- Do the captions interpret, sell, and lead the evaluator to the proper conclusion?
- Are long fold-outs minimized?
- Are visuals vertical rather than horizontal, introduced in prior text, and numbered correctly and sequentially?

The vertical review team for text reworks the text, ignoring the themes and the visuals. This team asks:
- Is the text well-organized, using the four-box organizational approach?
- Are section introductions reflected in sub-headings?
- Is the writing customer-focused? Does the text sell by linking benefits to features, in that order?
- Is plenty of white space used (bulleted lists, one-sentence paragraphs, boxes, changes in type size) to aid the reader and emphasize major points?
- Is the writing clear and consistent?

The volume leaders and section writers revise text as necessary, and the editors re-edit the revised drafts and submit them for production. Well-organized proposal materials are easier to evaluate, prompt fewer follow-up questions, and better support contract negotiations.

82 — Conduct final compliance check and *publish* proposal deliverables

82
Conduct final compliance check and "publish" proposal deliverables

See ELECTRONIC SUBMITTAL *and* PRODUCTION, *Proposal Guide.*

The core team should check the compliance of the entire proposal. Use the compliance checklist and cross-reference matrix to verify 100-percent compliance unless you have deliberately opted to submit a non-compliant solution.

Conduct a "page-turn" review after final reproduction and assembly to determine if any pages passed through reproduction off center or if any pages did not print. Minimize the embarrassment of finding errors after you ship the proposal.

Check CDs to make sure they are readable on various computers; prepared in the customer's preferred software, version, and operating system; comply with file size limitations, and are virus free. Do the graphics and text appear as intended? Submit in Portable Document Format (PDF) when permitted. If not, embed the fonts used to eliminate awkward font substitutions.

With electronic submissions increasingly becoming the norm, complete similar checks and processes before uploading to FTP sites.

83 — Conduct final legal, cost, and management reviews; hold Gold Team

83
Conduct final legal, cost, and management reviews; hold Gold Team

See COLOR TEAM REVIEWS, *Capture Guide.*

A proposal involves more than just setting forth your design for the finest *widget* the customer could ever hope to find. Depending on the customer, proposals in the competitive range or the winning proposal will be the basis for negotiations that lead to a legally binding contract. Submit every proposal for a legal review unless you are proposing standard products and services with pre-approved terms and conditions.

The Gold Team reviews the final version of the proposal. It confirms improvements recommended by Red and Green Teams have been incorporated. Proposal document quality and conformance to organizational standards are verified. In summary, the Gold Team determines whether the sales document is ready for the Proposal Submittal decision, where final authorization will be obtained to deliver it to the customer. A properly conducted Gold Team lets the executive focus on the deal at the decision gate rather than the document.

Milestones

- Gold Team

84 — Submit proposal

84
Submit proposal

Submit the proposal on time. Plan a backup delivery method in case something goes awry.

For electronic submissions, have an IT (Information Technology) expert available to help with potential transmission glitches. Get a time stamp on electronic submittals.

When using couriers, insist on a receipt of delivery with a time stamp. Couriers will get these for you if asked. When delivering in person, have one made that the receiving individual can sign.

Milestones

- Proposal submittal

Documents and Results

- Final proposal for delivery

Post-Submittal Activities

Post-Submittal Activities are about closing the sale as rapidly as possible so you can begin converting your business development success into revenue and bottom-line profit. Clarify and resolve open items, enter and promptly conclude contract negotiations, and then plan and initiate a smooth transition to service delivery.

Having expended 85 percent of the capture costs by proposal submittal, close the sale by immediately focusing on post-submittal activities (see figure 36). Develop discussion and pricing strategies that reinforce your strengths and mitigate your weaknesses.

Convince the customer that you care about this contract and will be responsive to the customer's needs and requirements. While some key capture participants might be reassigned, maintain a consistent leader and focus on the customer.

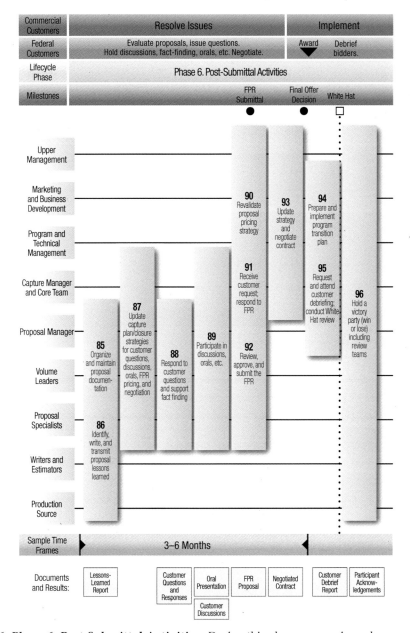

Figure 36. Phase 6: Post-Submittal Activities. *During this phase, engage in exchanges with the customer on Evaluation Notices (ENs), answering clarification questions, justifying your inclusion in the competitive range, and negotiating or holding discussions that lead to a Final Proposal Revision (FPR). Approximately 15 percent of the total BD cost is spent after initial proposal submission.*

85

85
Organize
and maintain
proposal
documen-
tation

See PRODUCTION,
Proposal Guide.

Organize and maintain proposal documentation

Collect all relevant materials used to produce the proposal as well as finished copies of the entire proposal. These materials will be needed for the FPR, negotiations, and potential protests or post-award delivery activities. As shown in figure 37, organize them so they are readily available as you move toward program execution.

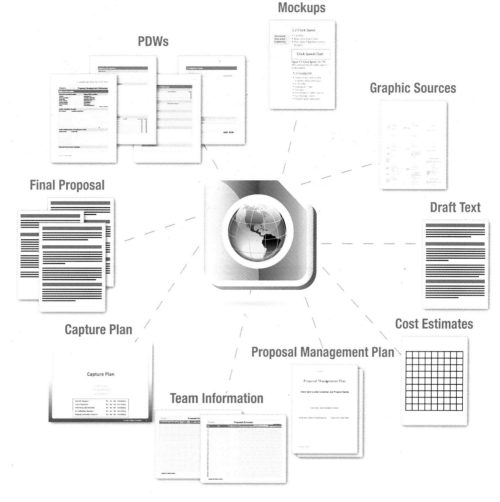

Figure 37. Program and Proposal Archives. *Organized, accessible program and proposal archives reduce problems during post-submittal activities, including cost proposal audits. Ideally, capture and proposal leaders and contributors are available, but memories are incomplete, unsupported, and often challenged, so these archived materials are essential to negotiate the contract and minimize your programmatic and technical risk.*

86

86
Identify, write,
and transmit
proposal
lessons
learned

See COLOR TEAM
REVIEWS, *Capture
Guide.*

Identify, write, and transmit proposal lessons learned

Conduct a *lessons learned* review to determine how your processes, strategies, and talent can be improved. Conduct this review as soon as possible after proposal submittal while memories are fresh and before capture and proposal team contributors are unavailable or less interested.

The first focus is on your internal successes, problems, and improvements. The second is from an external perspective to identify ways future pursuits can be more successful.

87

87
Update
capture
plan/closure
strategies
for customer
questions,
discussions,
orals, FPR
pricing, and
negotiation

See ENGAGING PROGRAM
MANAGEMENT,
PRESENTATIONS TO
CUSTOMERS, *and* PRICING
TO WIN, *Capture
Guide*; ORAL PROPOSALS,
Proposal Guide.

Update capture plan/closure strategies for customer questions, discussions, orals, FPR pricing, and negotiation

Many customers, including governments, conduct discussions with bidders before making a final award decision. These may lead to proposal modifications (called Final Proposal Revisions by the U.S. federal government). The strategy for the revision discussion is usually based on three things:

- The capture triumvirate's sense of the proposal's strengths and weaknesses
- The questions and clarifications you received and answered
- Intelligence gathered since submitting the proposal (including competitive information)

Overall, the strategy should be fairly simple:

- To respond fully to customer questions and concerns
- To reinforce customer's trust in your solution and organization

Typically, the members of the customer's staff who meet with organization personnel during the discussion come either from the customer's program office—those who will conduct the program—or from the group that evaluated the proposals. Prepare for these meetings much like preparing for an oral proposal presentation. Determine who should participate and define each participant's role.

Your team must appear to be technically competent and well-managed. Prepare to explain the cost-estimating methods or cost-accounting techniques. Provide sound answers to their technical, program management, and key personnel questions without overwhelming them with details. Over-answering questions often leads to more questions that might not support your strategy and position.

Refine and reconfirm your strategy before entering discussions. Address these questions:.

- What questions will the customer ask?
- Who on the team will answer which questions?
- How should you answer these questions?
- What should you emphasize in your responses?
- What should you say when you do not have an answer?
- What things do you want to say regardless of what questions the customer asks?
- What things do you want to say before and after the meeting?
- What things do you not want to say?
- What things do you want to discover?
- How technical should you be?

- Who will take notes during the meeting?
- How will you get this information back to the writers for the rewrites?
- What documents and *things* do you need to take?
- How should the team dress?

Carefully select discussion team members. Balance technical competence and communication skills. Take people who are professional, articulate, and knowledgeable about their area of expertise—technical, management, cost, and production.

Use the rehearsal of the discussion to screen people. Select 3-6 people to meet the customer. While most participants should be experts in a defined area, every participant should be familiar with the customer, program, your solution, and your strategy.

Rehearse discussions. A disorganized, inarticulate, poorly-managed team suggests that you will deliver the solution in a similar fashion.

Follow these suggestions when rehearsing:

- Have a high-level manager ask the questions that the customer is expected to ask.
- Ask difficult, challenging questions.
- Have the selected team members dress as they would for the real discussion.
- If possible, videotape the session and have the team members review and critique it afterwards.
- Review previously videotaped sessions, if available.
- Prepare your negotiation plan

A negotiation plan prepares you to negotiate the final contract with the customer. In many business negotiations, the negotiator loses sight of the goal, pushes too far, and loses the opportunity to achieve the initial goal. Successful negotiations are often 80 percent preparation and 20 percent execution.

Prior to entering a negotiation, identify your interests and those of your customer. Develop clear criteria to evaluate and measure options posed by either party. Successful negotiators establish a zone of potential agreement, setting high and low outcomes objectives. Consider the following facets:

- Understand the value of the potential deal to you and the customer.
- Secure the support of your management and teammates on the parameters of an acceptable deal.

See Value Proposition, *Capture Guide.*

- Quantify your bargaining range: minimum acceptable, target, opening position, and estimate of the customer's opening and acceptable position.
- Determine your leverage, a function of your strengths and weaknesses, and your customer's strengths and weaknesses. Quantify the value of these strengths, weaknesses, and discriminators to help you assess the impact of potential concessions.

- Develop a preferred agenda, listing issues, in order, that you and your customer will want to discuss.
- Identify potential ethical issues and how you might resolve them.

88

88
Respond to customer questions and support fact finding

See Pricing to Win, *Capture Guide.*

Respond to customer questions and support fact finding

When customers do not fully understand a proposal, they may communicate with bidders or ask questions. These may be called Errors, Omissions, and Clarifications; Clarification Requests (CRs); Deficiency Reports (DRs); Contractor Inquiries; or Evaluation Notices (ENs). Whatever the name, they stand for the same thing: parts of the proposal that the evaluators do not understand, find confusing, or believe they do not have sufficient information to evaluate accurately.

Customers may communicate in written or oral form. They ask you to respond in writing, in a presentation, or both.

Treat such questions seriously and respond in the most appropriate manner with the best information available. They are usually written by evaluators, so when responding to them, you are responding to a question posed by an evaluator.

Follow these guidelines:

- Log the question as it is received and forward it to selected members of the program office and proposal project team.
- Analyze questions as carefully as the RFP. Respond fully and on time. If questions are long or complicated, create compliance checklists for each one.

- Outline your response with a group of relevant core team members, including the section author, volume manager, and technical or management content expert.
- If a discussion follows the written responses, keep track of all questions by topic area and develop an aligned discussion strategy. The questions indicate where the customer had concerns with the proposal; the same issues are usually raised during discussions.
- Do not respond by referring the customer to the proposal. Instead, answer the question, confirm that your answer was sufficient, and only then might you refer them to proposal content that was difficult to locate.
- Maintain a helpful, professional tone in your written and oral responses. Your objective is to enhance your position.
- Be sure that the cost volume leader is aware of the technical questions. The technical areas in question may have some bearing on the pricing strategy and could influence the price quoted in any proposal revision. The customer's fact-finding objective is to clarify the proposal but not to reach an agreement. Fact finding may be done by the customer's cost analyst, the field auditors, or technical auditors.

Documents and Results

- Customer questions and responses

89

89
Participate in discussions, orals, etc.

See Oral Proposals, *Proposal Guide.*

Participate in discussions, orals, etc.

Ideally, your proposal secured a contract award. But when, as frequently happens, the customer wants to talk first, organization representatives should:

- Be warm and friendly but not chummy.
- Be professional but not cold.
- Speak confidently, but do not sound cocky or arrogant.
- Use subtle humor, but do not tell a joke.

- Praise your strengths, but do not brag.
- Answer questions directly, without windy introductions, prefaces, forewords, or qualifications.
- Do not over-answer questions.

Documents and Results

- Oral presentation
- Customer discussions

90

90
Revalidate
proposal
pricing
strategy

See Pricing to Win,
Capture Guide.

Revalidate proposal pricing strategy

Following discussions, the team should have a better sense of how your price compares with alternative solutions. Before revising your proposal, review the pricing strategy by answering these questions:

- Will your prices stay the same?
- Will you re-scope the job, adapt your approach, or modify your profit margin?
- Will you adapt your prices in response to competitors' probable strategies?

- Will you discount something? Offer a price guarantee? Provide a warranty? Improve the warranty?

Remember: the lowest price bidder, especially if it has a good BOE formula, will be the yardstick against which all other bidders are compared. However, you do not want to win a contract that you cannot support, fulfill, or afford to accept.

91

91
Receive
customer
request;
respond to
FPR

See Pricing to Win,
Capture Guide.

Receive customer request; respond to FPR

After reviewing the proposal, the customer often requests a proposal revision from each bidder. Write the revision just as the team wrote the original proposal. Mark each change so that the evaluators can find the changed material easily.

Use the original writers to make the changes if they are qualified, available, and needed. If changes are limited, volume leaders can often make and consolidate the changes.

Much like the initial proposal writing process, schedule a color team review of the revised proposal.

Make only those changes that the customer specifically requests or comments on. Never make unnecessary changes. Evaluators review only your changes, so changes to other sections will not be considered.

92

92
Review,
approve, and
submit the
FPR

Review, approve, and submit the FPR

Reconvene the Red Team to review the revision. Review meticulously because these changes will be carefully reviewed by the customer. This Red Team must make sure that you have responded fully to the customer's questions and have incorporated the desired strategy.

Milestones

- FPR submittal

Documents and Results

- FPR proposal

93

93
Update
strategy
and
negotiate
contract

Update strategy and negotiate contract

You have not won until you sign the contract. Negotiation changes an average marketplace to a specific marketplace. Negotiation changes averages and assumptions to reality.

Planning is essential in preparing and conducting negotiations. Both parties can win, but the unprepared negotiator is at a severe disadvantage.

Develop your negotiation strategy based on a thorough understanding of the government's goals, issues, requirements, and the current situation. Base your negotiation strategy on the intelligence documented in your capture plan.

Keep three items in mind when developing your negotiation strategy:

- What the RFP requires
- What you have promised in the proposal
- What requirements the customer might want to change

You might be asked to negotiate if you are in the competitive range, but you probably will not know how you rank with your competitors. Ask. Sometimes the customer will tell.

Despite the rhetoric about seeking a *fair and reasonable* price, government negotiators are always seeking a lower price once requirements are met. They will be well-prepared to challenge specific cost areas.

See Pricing to Win, *Capture Guide.*

Check your facts, prepare your solution approach and justification, have a distinct negotiation objective, anticipate arguments the government will use, and develop responses to these arguments.

Usually, the program manager and contracts personnel negotiate. The capture or proposal manager might be involved as an advisor because of his/her RFP and proposal knowledge. His/her principal job is to ensure that the program manager and the contracts people do not contradict the proposal, the RFP, or "good business practice."

One member of the cost volume team should be on the negotiating team, or make sure the negotiator understands the cost data. While purchasing regulations restrict changes in requirements without reopening the competition, expect subtle changes or "clarifications" in requirements.

Seemingly small changes in design or schedule could make major differences in production, personnel, and costs. Carefully analyze the impact of changes before you accept them.

Milestones (between Steps 93 and 94)
- Final Offer Decision

Documents and Results
- Negotiated contract

---

94 Prepare and implement program transition plan

94
Prepare and implement program transition plan

See Engaging Program Support, *Capture Guide.*

The proposed program transition plan is frequently modified by the negotiated terms of the awarded contract. Actual transition plans must be quickly prepared from the baseline of the proposed plan, reflecting new contract requirements.

Typical content of a transition plan includes:

- Planned contract start and end dates
- Deliverables, milestones, due dates, review types and dates, and approval procedures
- If onsite with customer: office fixture inventory, removal or placement, badging or other access, services connect or disconnect (telephones, copier maintenance, etc.), parking facilities, copies of customer policies regarding proper individual conduct, emergency provisions, inclement weather situations, etc.

- Classified materials inventory and transfer of custody
- Customer contact lists: key personnel, fax numbers, e-mail addresses, working hours, etc
- Billing formats and deadlines
- Customer accounts receivable contacts.
- Databases to be maintained
- Hardware and software to be implemented or maintained, including upgrade and backup considerations
- Scheduling of key personnel (if resumes of key individuals were included in the proposal, their availability should be solidified. You do not want to promise the customer something that you cannot deliver)
- In-briefings and out-briefings for key personnel (e.g., security officer)

95

95
Request
and attend
customer
debriefing;
conduct White
Hat review

See Pricing to Win, *Capture Guide.*

Request and attend customer debriefing; conduct White Hat review

Win or lose, always request and attend a debriefing by the customer. You have nothing to lose, and you may gain a lot.

U.S. federal regulations permit bidders to request either a pre-award or a post-award debrief, but not both. Request a pre-award debrief only if you believe an error in the announced evaluation process has been made, and you intend to file a protest.

Request a debrief to help your organization and team improve future proposals and build a positive relationship with the customer. One caveat regarding the debriefing is that other criteria might override the merits of the proposal, the technical quality of the product, or even the cost.

If you lost, learn from your mistakes. The same people may evaluate your next proposal, so do not be defensive or argumentative. You probably will not agree with all of their criticisms of your proposal. But remember your role—they are the evaluators, and you are the evaluatee.

Customer debriefs on winning proposals are often the most useful. Hopefully, you will be able to repeat the processes and characteristics that led to the win.

Add the input from your customer debrief to the White Hat review, where you review from both internal and external perspectives ways that future pursuits can be more successful. The White Hat review can be a key component of continuous process improvement for your organization's business development operations.

White Hat reviews gather information from both internal and external participants in an opportunity pursuit. They should document things that worked well and those that did not. They should develop recommendations, including steps and activities to continue and methods or approaches to change. All available information should be honestly assessed for understanding.

Milestones

- White Hat

Documents and Results

- Customer debrief report

96

96
Hold a
victory
party (win
or lose)
including
review
teams

Hold a victory party (win or lose), including review teams

Have a victory party for all individuals who contributed to the proposal. While this step is at the end, many proposal managers hold the first victory party immediately after proposal submittal, and then schedule a second victory party if they win the contract.

Your team has worked hard and put in long hours, often sacrificing personal or family time and responsibilities. Recognize their efforts, accomplishments, and value to your organization. Contributors who feel appreciated are more inclined to support subsequent proposal efforts.

Documents and Results

- Participant acknowledgements

Adapt the descriptions of business development team roles and responsibilities to your market sector, organization, resources, and typical opportunities.

Distinguish roles and positions. An individual might assume multiple roles but usually occupies a single organizational position. Roles and positions usually overlap. For example, a person might be in a proposal manager position but assume capture manager, proposal manager, and proposal writer roles.

Assigning one person to multiple roles is often necessary due to limited resources, but you risk neglecting vital tasks due to limited time or breadth of talent.

If you engage a business development consultant, the roles and responsibilities of the consultant differ from an employee, even when they carry the same title. Engage a consultant when you lack the capability and/ or capacity to fill the roles needed to win an opportunity. The best consultants are highly skilled and capable of fulfilling multiple roles but not necessarily every role required.

Begin each consulting engagement with a clear mutual understanding of the expected role, capabilities, responsibilities, and limitations of the consultant.

Capture Manager

A capture manager is charged with capturing a specific business opportunity, usually by managing a capture team. The capture manager identifies the resources needed to pursue a business opportunity; oversees capture, teaming, pricing, and proposal strategies; and manages the transitions from opportunity positioning to proposal development, negotiation, award, and program initiation.

The capture manager owns the deal, from initial assignment as the capture manager for a qualified lead to transition to execution of the contract. The capture manager completes or manages the following tasks:

- Populate, validate, update, and implement capture plan.
- Plan, document, and manage the internal and external capture project efforts.
- Brief executive management as scheduled.
- Align marketing intelligence with the capture strategy.
- Assess customer's issues, program requirements, and competitive position.
- Conduct, manage, or obtain competitive and price-to-win analysis.

- Collaboratively develop capture strategy with the program manager and proposal manager.
- Serve as primary point of contact among the proposal development, solution, and pricing team.
- Secure senior management commitment and corporate resources for capture and proposal efforts.
- Monitor, review, and direct weekly proposal progress, ensuring adherence to the proposal process and schedule.
- Manage the capture triumvirate, comprising the capture, program, and proposal managers.
- Develop the initial executive summary draft; direct completion of the final version; and confirm alignment among the executive summary, volume summaries, and customer presentations.
- Participate as an independent proposal evaluator in all major proposal reviews.
- Prepare and present the capture plan at the Pursuit, Bid, and Bid Validation Decision Gate reviews.
- Participate in color team reviews.

Proposal Manager

A proposal manager is charged with preparing a winning proposal. The proposal manager develops the proposal management plan and manages to that plan. The capture manager owns the deal, from initial assignment as the capture manager for a qualified lead to transition to execution of the contract.

The proposal manager completes or manages the following tasks:

- Support the sales lead/capture manager by managing and directing proposal preparation tasks and personnel.
- Prepare the proposal management plan.
- Transform capture strategy into aligned proposal strategies and themes.
- Direct development of the proposal outline, confirm compliance with the bid request, and use it as a key proposal configuration control medium.
- Analyze the RFP, and allocate proposal requirements against the proposal outline to prepare a compliant and responsive proposal.
- Build the proposal compliance matrix and track fulfillment of all requirements.
- Review storyboards, graphics, and section drafts to ensure requirements are adequately addressed within page allocations.

- Conduct regular proposal progress status meetings, and maintain the proposal schedule.
- Develop a Pink Team (storyboard review) plan for the interim review and internal evaluation of the technical, management, cost, and past performance volumes and additional required submittals.
- Direct writing, editing, and rewriting efforts to achieve a persuasive, customer-focused, clear, and concise proposal.
- Work with the volume leaders to achieve inter-volume compatibility.
- Develop a Red Team review plan and support the Red Team review lead.
- Assess Red Team review recommendations with the capture triumvirate, and incorporate approved recommendations into the final proposal.
- Direct the proposal coordinator's configuration control and proposal production activities.
- Complete reasonable and normal duties associated with the proposal manager position, as directed by the business development, capture, or proposal center managers.

Orals Coach

An orals coach is tasked with preparing the briefing team to present a winning oral proposal. An orals coach orchestrates the oral proposal presentation or finals briefing by guiding the development of the presentation and then coaching individuals and the team to present a winning proposal.

Orals coaches are frequently engaged as consultants because few organizations can justify them as a full-time position. The orals coach completes or manages the following tasks:

Development (Message and Strategy) Consulting

- Oversee integration and alignment of the *capture strategy* into the orals presentation strategy.
- Create presentation outline.
- Facilitate content development brainstorming sessions.

- Guide presentation storyboarding, aligning customer issues and solution features using graphics, layout, and branding elements.
- Meet with proposal section authors and topic briefers to integrate proposal and presentations themes for consistency and customer focus.
- Establish oral presentation development timelines and milestones.
- Schedule and facilitate strategy and content review sessions with capture, proposal, and executive management teams.
- Integrate compliance matrices and bidders comparison data into the orals presentation.
- Coordinate with proposal manager and key team members to maintain inter-volume and section consistency.
- Develop powerful introduction, support for main points, and conclusion.

Orals Delivery Coaching

- Help select presentation team.
- Define presentation standards and presentation roles.
- Determine appropriate, persuasive, and effective support mediums for the presentation.
- Rehearse and coach individual presenters on presentation style, including verbal and non-verbal messages, voice, eye contact, posture, and movement.

- Coach individuals to present clearly, concisely, and persuasively.
- Facilitate team presentation practice, peer-review, and dress rehearsal sessions.
- Anticipate and rehearse how to field, assign, answer, and summarize customer questions and discussions.
- Help orchestrate the oral presentation event – logistics, room set-up, technology, etc.
- Build confidence and credibility within the presentation team.

Volume Manager/Leader

The volume manager is tasked with preparing a compliant, responsive, highly evaluated proposal volume. The volume manager or leader coaches section writers and contributors to prepare compliant and responsive proposal sections on schedule that conform with the proposal outline, compliance matrix, and quality standards.

The volume manager completes or manages the following tasks:

- Assist the proposal manager in developing outlines, response matrices.
- Manage writers' completion of Proposal Development Worksheets (PDWs) or storyboards.
- Provide Just-In-Time training and assistance to section writers and subject matter experts (SMEs) in creating proposal storyboards, graphics, and text inputs.
- Lead and direct all efforts required to produce the volume as dictated by the RFP and proposal manager.

- Track and report daily status of volume development to the proposal manager.
- Identify volume requirement issues, suggest compliant solutions, and implement in proposal volume and supporting documentation.
- Review and edit volume sections as necessary.
- Enforce page limits or guidelines, document and page design styles, and similar requirements.
- Prepare detailed Red Team evaluation plan and materials for the volume.
- Direct the incorporation of accepted volume-specific Red Team comments.
- Ensure final volume master copy quality control.
- Support production of final volume copies for delivery.
- Complete reasonable and normal task as directed by the proposal manager.

Technical/Proposal Writer

The proposal writer is tasked to produce a compliant, responsive, customer-focused, highly evaluated proposal section. The primary emphasis is on the ability to organize and present clear, persuasive content either from personal knowledge or by obtaining input from subject matter experts (SME).

The proposal writer completes or manages the following tasks:

- Identify, research if necessary, and understand section response requirements from the response matrix and bid request.

- Identify relevant company proposal materials, applicable boilerplate, and intelligence that might be adapted to the writing assignment.
- Develop PDWs or proposal section storyboards using the proposal outline and compliance matrix.
- Mockup proposal section and draft proposal text.
- Review, revise, and edit of proposal graphics and text.
- Edit electronic and hard copy proposal drafts, Red Team, and final versions as directed by the proposal manager.

- Maintain contextual integrity of proposal sections by coordinating edits with the respective SME/contributor.
- Assist proposal coordinator or production manager in maintaining version control at each review and edit stage through final document *freeze*.

- Assist the proposal coordinator in the production, reproduction, and binding/packaging of proposal hard and soft copies.
- Complete reasonable and normal duties associated with the proposal writer/editor position, as directed by the proposal or volume leader.

Desktop Publisher

The desktop publisher formats text, numerical data, charts, graphs, and photographs within a common style sheet to produce a cohesive, easy-to-read and evaluate proposal. The desktop publisher completes or manages the following tasks:

- Assist the proposal/production coordinator in establishing and maintaining electronic proposal files.
- Develop and document submission/transmission protocols for proposal inputs, backup, archiving, and printing.
- Develop writers' guidance for submittal, transmission, and filing of all hard and soft copy proposal inputs.
- Establish the proposal style sheets and templates for soft and printed copy proposal masters.

- Format proposal text and integrate graphic files to produce iterative hard copy section drafts, review team hard/soft copies, and the final proposal master.
- Maintain daily backup, version control, and archive proposal hard/soft copy inputs.
- Integrate, format, and publish draft, review team, and final versions as directed by production coordinator.
- Assist in the reproduction and binding/packaging of proposal versions.
- Produce proposal volume soft copies as required by the customer.
- Complete reasonable and normal duties associated with the desktop publisher position as directed by the proposal coordinator or manager.

Graphic Specialist

The graphic specialist develops, modifies, and coordinates proposal graphic elements to achieve visual consistency and clarity. The graphic specialist completes or manages the following tasks:

- Establish the graphic software standards and transportability for graphic inputs.
- Assist the proposal coordinator in establishing electronic graphic file protocols, tracking for proposal configuration control, tracking status, and maintaining document integrity.
- Develop the writers' guidance for transmission and archiving hard/soft copy proposal graphic inputs.
- Help contributors develop graphic concepts to communicate key concepts clearly and persuasively in storyboards and drafts.

- Edit, polish, and convert contributors' graphics to selected graphics formats for review, approval, and desktop publishing.
- Assist desktop publishers in the placement and integration of text and graphic files for proposal reviews and final production.
- Assist in the reproduction, binding, and packaging of proposal volumes for reviews and delivery to the customer.
- Incorporate graphic files into deliverable soft copies as required by the RFP.
- Complete reasonable and normal duties associated with the graphic specialist position, as directed by the proposal coordinator or manager.

Proposal Editor

The proposal editor works with the proposal team to improve the quality, clarity, organization, customer focus, and persuasiveness of the writing. The proposal editor focuses on making the text clear, concise, and correct.

The proposal editor completes or manages the following tasks:

- Impose the four-box organization on text at all levels.
- Edit proposal sections for grammar, style, consistency, and correctness.
- Improve the readability and clarity of text by using active voice and concise language, eliminating gobbledygook, and minimizing jargon.
- Minimize style differences from multiple authors and contributors.

- Improve customer focus by placing benefits before features, linking benefits to features, and naming the customer before the seller.
- Align summaries, introductions, informative subheadings, theme statements, action captions, and graphics with the proposal strategy.
- Ensure the proper contextual integrity of each completed proposal section by reviewing edits with the respective SME/contributor.
- Maintain version control at each review stage from draft to final document *freeze*.
- Complete reasonable and normal duties associated with the proposal editor position as directed by the volume manager, proposal manager, or proposal coordinator.

Proposal Coordinator

The proposal coordinator assists the proposal manager by coordinating administrative tasks that maintain the integrity and security of proposal information, inputs, and outputs.

The proposal coordinator completes or manages the following tasks:

- Help proposal manager prepare and maintain the proposal management plan, especially the proposal outline, schedule, and response matrix.
- Help the proposal manager prepare for the daily stand-up meeting.
- Help establish the proposal facility, hardware, and software.
- Establish the electronic and hard copy file structure, archive, and back-up capability and procedures for proposal materials.
- Establish and document electronic proposal file access and tracking protocols to maintain proposal documentation security and integrity.
- Establish and maintain storyboards (hard and soft copy).
- Control access to the proposal area and competition-sensitive or proprietary materials.

- Manage the production of draft and final text and graphics.
- Support proposal manager's development of proposal review plans, final production cycles, and required resources.
- Coordinate the internal flow and review of proposal inputs and outputs.
- Maintain real-time development status and version control of proposal text and graphics.
- Supervise the daily operations of graphic specialists and desktop publishers.
- Help proposal manager develop review team evaluation packages and then record, disseminate, and track accepted recommendations.
- Direct the production, reproduction, binding, and packaging of final master proposal and hard/soft copies.
- Secure or dispose of proposal assets and resources; sanitize the proposal facility upon delivery of the proposal.
- Complete reasonable and normal duties associated with the proposal coordinator position as directed by the proposal manager.

Contract Administrator

The contract administrator reviews bid request requirements and proposal commitments as the proposal is prepared, assists with contract negotiations, and then supports the program manager during delivery by ensuring that contracted services are delivered in conformance with requirements.

The contract administrator completes or manages the following tasks:

- Review bid request requirements for unique, unusual, non-standard terms, conditions, and requirements.
- Review, analyze, and proactively administer the contract to determine obligations and confirm compliance.
- Identify, research, and analyze applicable contract acquisition regulations, guidelines, and requirements.
- Identify contractual transition and performance risks.

- Respond to customer, teaming partner, subcontractor, and vendor contractual inquiries.
- Draft nondisclosure, teaming, and subcontracting agreements.
- Contribute to pre-contract discussions, negotiations, and contract changes.
- Monitor company conformance with proposal and contractual requirements, terms and conditions, identify problems, alert program management, and monitor corrections.
- Prepare and disseminate information to program management regarding contract status, compliance, modifications, deviations, negotiations, and completion or termination.
- Identify and document contract-specific lessons learned and best practices for capture, proposal, and program management teams.

Cost Volume Manager

The cost volume manager ensures that the cost volume complies with the bid request and conforms to organizational directives regarding the proposal process, outline, and compliance matrix.

The cost volume manager completes or manages the following tasks:

- Assist the proposal manager in developing cost volume outlines, response matrices, and Proposal Development Worksheets (PDWs).
- Prepare a cost volume summary, aligned with the proposal executive summary.
- Provide Just-In-Time, cost-specific guidance and training.
- Direct writers, cost and pricing analysts, and estimators in creating task descriptions, estimates, rationale, cost volume storyboards, graphics, and text inputs.
- Direct development of costing and pricing assumptions.

- Lead and direct development of a reasonable, realistic, and trackable cost volume as dictated by the bid request.
- Track and report status of the cost volume development on a daily basis to the proposal manager.
- Resolve cost volume requirement issues and suggest compliant costing/pricing documentation.
- Review and edit cost volume sections.
- Enforce or impose page limitations, styles, and other requirements.
- Prepare the cost volume for each color team review.
- Incorporate accepted color team review recommendations.
- Maintain alignment between the cost volume and the rest of the proposal.
- Ensure quality control for the final cost volume master copy (both electronic and paper).
- Prepare, with administrative support, the final cost volume copies (electronic and paper) for delivery.

IMP/IMS Specialist

The IMP/IMS specialist manages the preparation of the Integrated Master Plan (IMP) and Integrated Master Schedule (IMS) to ensure that the program can be completed within schedule and cost constraints, and minimizes risk related with the WBS and SOW.

The IMP/IMS specialist completes or manages the following tasks:

- Ensure the IMP is an event-oriented representation of integrated product and services development—each activity includes related tasks for that activity.

- Create list of measured, scheduled events.

- Document assumptions, guidelines, and definitions of action verbs used to describe events.

- Maintain version control.

- Link all IMP and IMS events.

- Identify secondary tasks, boundaries, and owners.

- Identify task links and interdependencies for critical path analysis.

Price-to-Win Specialist

The price-to-win specialist assesses the competition, competitors' prior strategies, trend data, public domain costing and pricing data, and the customer's requirements, estimates, and buying trends to identify a probable winning price window. The price-to-win specialist provides an independent perspective and input to the capture manager and executive management as they progress through decision gate reviews and develop a winning solution at an acceptable price.

The price-to-win specialist completes or manages the following tasks:

- Understand the price/capability trade-off.

- Gather and analyze publicly available data in compliance with the standards of Strategic and Competitive Intelligence Professionals (SCIP)

- Develop, build, and maintain a competitive assessment database.

- Determine relevant costing and pricing alternatives.

- Determine the customer's budget, funding profile, and independent cost estimate.

- Estimate the lowest-cost, marginally compliant solution; the capability-satisfied solution; and the value-driven solution to bound or describe the winning price-capability window.

- Help the capture team prepare a capture strategy that incorporates the competitive assessment in the pursuit and capture planning phases, and price to win in the proposal planning and development phases of business development.

- Recommend strategic and tactical solution modifications to the capture manager that improve the win probability.

- Repeatedly update the price-to-win assessment from the pursuit to the award decision gate reviews.

Program Manager

The program manager is tasked with delivering the contracted services and products in accordance with the contract, satisfy the customer, and meet the business objectives of the selling organization. The program manager owns the solution pre-contract and implements the solution post-award.

The program manager completes or manages the following business development tasks:

- Develop the solution. If services oriented, the program manager focuses on the management and service delivery aspects. If the solution is highly technical, integrate the engineering or technical team solution and the program management and infrastructure support aspects of the solution.
- Discuss solution facets, alternatives, and tradeoffs with the customer as requirements are developed and finalized.
- Refine the potential solution during capture planning, proposal planning, and proposal development.
- Identify potential program risks and develop risk management and mitigation alternatives.
- Identify, recruit, and obtain the commitment of key program delivery personnel.

- Guide and support writers and contributors as they prepare proposal sections.
- Review and confirm the alignment of proposal sections describing the proposed solution.
- Oversee preparation of the Contract Work Breakdown Structure (CWBS), discussion of work share, and cost estimates.
- Coordinate program-specific contributions of teammates, subcontractors, and vendors.
- Support decision gate and color team reviews.
- Lead oral proposal team presentation, with emphasis on delivery team management, customer interface, and reporting.
- Assume a lead capture triumvirate role post-submittal, leading discussions and contract negotiations.
- Identify, define, position, propose, and capture additional post-award contract task additions and modifications.

Note: The program manager's post-award direct program management tasks and responsibilities are not included.

Appendix B: Acronyms *The acronyms shown are limited to those used in this Lifecycle Guide.*

APMP	Association of Proposal Management Professionals	**IPPT**	Integrated Product and Process Team
BD	Business Development	**IPT**	Integrated Product Team
B&P	Bid and Proposal	**IT**	Information Technology
BOE	Basis of Estimate	**LPTA**	Lowest Price Technically Acceptable
CAIV	Cost as an Independent Variable	**OPP**	Oral Proposal Planner
CDRL	Contract Data Requirements List	**PCO**	Procurement Contracting Officer
CLIN	Contract Line Item Number	**PDW**	Proposal Development Worksheet
CR	Clarification Request	**PMP**	Proposal Management Plan
DoD	Department of Defense	**R & D**	Research and Development
DR	Deficiency Report	**RFI**	Request For Information
EN	Evaluation Notice	**RFP**	Request for Proposal
EOC	Error, Omission, Clarification	**RFT**	Request For Tender
FAR	Federal Acquisition Regulations	**RFQ**	Request for Quote
FCDR	Final Critical Design Review	**ROM**	Rough Order of Magnitude
FOIA	Freedom of Information Act	**SME**	Subject Matter Expert
FPR	Final Proposal Review and Final Proposal Revision	**SOO**	Statement of Objectives
FTP	File Transfer Protocol	**SOW**	Statement of Work
ICDR	Interim, Internal, or Intermediate Critical Design Review	**SSA**	Source Selection Authority
ICE	Independent Cost Estimate	**SSEB**	Source Selection Evaluation Board
IDIQ	Indefinite Delivery Indefinite Quality	**WBS**	Work Breakdown Structure
IMP	Integrated Master Plan	**WPW**	Winning Price Window
IMS	Integrated Master Schedule		

Appendix C: Interactive Business Development Lifecycle™ Tool

Shipley's 96-step business development process and framework are available by subscription as an interactive, web-based tool. Use it to access descriptions of each phase and step in the lifecycle, integrated with topic sections of the *Shipley Capture Guide* and *Shipley Proposal Guide*.

Access the online business development chart via this link:

http://sbdl.shipleywins.com

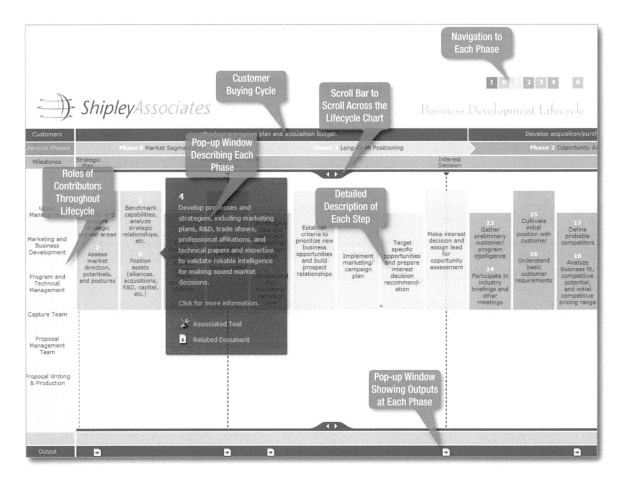

Index

A

Account plans, 4, 16
Action caption, 49, 50, 54, 69
Action plans, 17, 18, 19
Active voice, 69
Addressable budget, 20
Award, 65

B

Backup delivery method, 55
Bargaining range, 59
Baseline, 25
Baseline design, 39
Baseline offering, 33
Baseline solution, 22, 29, 38
Benchmark, 2
Benefits, 53, 69
Best value, 20, 34
Bid and Proposal (B&P), 24, 48
Bid decision, 29, 43, 48
Bid Decision Gate review, 14, 65
   bid request, 30, 42, 66, 70
   bid validation, 44
Bid Validation Decision Gate review,
      26, 42, 43, 44, 46, 65
   bid/no-bid recommendation, 25, 43
Bidder Comparison Chart, 18, 29, 53
Bidders comparison data, 66
Bidders' Conference, 29
Black Hat review, 19, 22
Blue Team review, 19
BOE (Basis of Estimate), 38, 49, 60
Boilerplate, 29, 67
Brainstorming, 36
Budget, 16, 18, 28
Business case, 11, 24
Business fit, 12
Business-to-business customers, 16

C

Capital versus operating costs, 24
Capture, 6, 36, 43, 46, 49, 53, 57, 58, 61,
      66, 70
Capture core team, 15
Capture Guide, 74
Capture manager, 9, 13, 14, 15, 18, 19,
      25, 27, 31, 36, 38, 45, 65, 66, 71
Capture plan, 13, 14, 17, 23, 25, 26, 31,
      53, 57, 58, 60
Capture Planning, 10, 11, 14, 16,
      19, 21
Capture planning template, 17, 23

Capture/proposal budget, 18
Capture strategy, 17, 19, 22, 25, 26, 27,
      39, 65, 66, 71
Capture team, 14, 20, 25, 71
Capture triumvirate, 13, 15, 16, 19, 58,
      89, 65, 66, 72
Contract Data Requirement List
      (CDRL), 37, 38, 42, 46, 52
Certifications and Representations, 33
Checklist, 47, 55
Clarification Requests (CRs), 59
Classified materials, 61
Color team reviews, 30, 48, 65, 70
Competitive, 30, 71
Competitive analysis, 17
Competitive intelligence, 11, 12, 20
Competitive pricing, 10, 20
Competitive pricing range, 12
Competitive range, 35
Competitor Intelligence, 18
Competitors, 2, 19, 24
Competitors' probable solutions, 22
Compliance, 29, 33, 41, 48, 51, 53, 55,
      66
   check, 37, 47, 55
   checklists, 29, 38, 42, 47, 48, 59
   matrix, 66, 67
   meetings, 51
Compliant, 25, 66, 67
Consistency, 51, 66, 69
Contingency Plan, 18
Contract, 59, 60, 61, 70, 72
Contract Administrator, 70
Contracting, 15
Contracting officer, 45
Contracting officer's technical repre-
      sentative, 45
Contract Line Item Numbers (CLINs),
      31, 32, 46
Contract negotiations, 54
Contractor inquiries, 59
Contracts, 61
Contracts manager, 31
Contract Work Breakdown Structure
      (CWBS), 72
Corporate competencies, 2
Corporate risks, 6
Cost, 18, 25, 29, 30, 31, 37, 51, 52, 55,
      71, 72
Cost-accounting techniques, 58
Cost as an Independent Variable
      (CAIV), 49
Cost bogies, 38
Cost drivers, 35

Cost estimates, 29, 57
Cost-estimating methods, 58
Costing, 51, 70, 71
Cost review, 52
Cost/schedule reports, 37
Cost volume, 51, 52, 53, 61, 66, 70
Cost volume leader, 35, 59
Cost volume manager, 30, 31, 37, 70
Couriers, 55
Cross-reference matrix, 31, 38, 55
Customer, 33
Customer analysis, 17
Customer Contact Plan, 18
Customer debriefing, 62
Customer focus, 23, 53, 54, 66, 69
Customer issues, 37
Customer's buying position, 20
Customer's requirements, 1, 11 16, 27,
      34, 41

D

Daily stand-up meeting, 69
Daily status meetings, 51
Data, 6
Data security, 36
Deadlines, 28
Debrief, 62
   for the proposal team, 53
Decision gate, 30, 72
Decision gate review, 12, 71
Decision makers, 6, 8, 11, 23, 50
Deficiency Reports (DRs), 59
Deliverables, 37, 42, 61
Design-freeze date, 46
Desktop publishing, 28, 29, 68, 69
Development, 66
Dictionary, 30
Discount, 60
Discriminators, 38, 39, 53, 59
Discussions, 59
Draft, 38
Draft PMP, 33
Draft RFP, 27, 31, 32, 34, 42, 43, 45,
      47, 48
Draft solicitation, 34
Dress rehearsal, 67

E

Edit, 28, 67, 68
Editing, 49, 66
Editors, 36, 54

Electronic submissions, 55
Engineers, 39
Errors, Omissions, and Clarifications, 59
Estimating, 37, 49
Estimators, 31, 37, 46, 49, 70
Ethical issues, 59
Evaluation, 62
Evaluation criteria, 32
Evaluation Notices (ENs), 56, 59
Evaluators, 47, 50, 53, 59, 60, 62
Executive summary, 18, 22, 23, 29, 38, 40, 42, 52, 65, 70

F

Favored position, 22
Features, 53, 66, 69
Features and benefits, 37, 38
Federal Acquisition Regulation (FAR), 20
Final bid/no-bid recommendation, 43
Final internal review, 48
Final Proposal Revision (FPR), 56, 57, 58, 60
Final RFP, 25, 27, 40, 43, 47
Finance, 15
Flowchart, 30, 33
Formal solicitation, 18
Format, 39
Four-box organization, 52, 69
Freedom of Information Act (FOIA), 12
Freeze the solution, 46
FTP sites, 55
Functional Responsibility matrix, 37
Funding, 24

G

Gantt chart, 48, 50
Gathering, 11
Ghost, 22
Gobbledygook, 69
Gold Team, 54, 55
Good writing, 32
Graphic artists specialists, 36, 50, 68, 69
Graphics, 28, 29, 37, 49, 50, 55, 57, 66, 67, 69, 70
Graphs, 68
Green Team, 53, 54
Guarantee, 60

H

Horizontal, 54
Horizontally (themes and visuals), 54
Hot buttons, 6, 8, 14, 18, 20, 22, 23, 32, 33
Hot button issues, 6

I

IMP/IMS Specialist, 71
Improved position, 18
Inch-stone, 29, 30, 44, 48, 51
Incumbent, 16, 22, 23, 24
Independent cost estimates (ICE), 20
Independent proposal evaluator, 65
Industry briefings, 11
Industry days, 11
Influencers, 11, 23, 50
In-house, 31
Initial, 65
Integrated Master Plan (IMP), 31, 46, 71
Integrated Master Schedule (IMS), 31, 46, 71
Integrated Product and Process Teams (IPPT), 49
Integrated Solution Worksheet, 18
Intelligence, 2, 3, 11, 14, 31, 34, 42, 45, 53, 58, 60, 65
Intelligence Collection Plan, 18
Intelligence gathering, 27
Interest decision, 8, 9
Interest Decision Gate review, 4, 5, 8, 9
Interest/no-interest recommendation package, 9

J

Jargon, 69
Just-In-Time training, 67, 70

K

Kickoff meeting, 29, 39, 44, 48, 49

L

Labor category, 50
Language, 18
Legal review, 55
Lessons learned, 16, 57
Leverage, 59
Library, 36
Long-Term Positioning, 5
Lowest Price Technically Acceptable (LPTA), 16, 20
Low price, 20

Low win probability, 8

M

Make/buy decision, 21
Make/buy plan, 31, 46
Management, 30, 33, 39, 70
    plans, 36
    proposal, 37
    requirements, 11
    reviews, 55
Management volume, 31, 45, 53, 66
Management volume managers, 30
Manager, 68
Market direction, 2
Marketers, 39
Marketing, 3
Marketing/campaign decision, 4
Marketing/Campaign Decision Gate review, 4, 6
Marketing/campaign plan, 3, 6, 8
Marketing/campaign recommendation package, 4
Market segment, 3, 12
MARKET SEGMENTATION, 1
Master program schedule, 31
Maximum justifiable capability, 20
Milestones, 28, 29, 37, 44, 48, 61, 66
Minimum acceptable capability, 20
Minimum price, 20
Mock evaluation, 53
Mockup, 23, 29, 36, 40, 41, 42, 49, 52, 57, 67
Must win, 7

N

Need to know, 48
Negotiate, 60
Negotiation Plan, 48, 58
Negotiations 57, 58, 60, 61, 65, 70, 72
Non-compliant, 55

O

Objectives, 3
Opportunity analysis report, 12
OPPORTUNITY ASSESSMENT, 10
Oral presentation, 59, 66, 67, 72
Oral proposal, 18
Oral Proposal Planner (OPP), 40, 42, 49
Orals, 58, 59
Orals Coach, 66
Organization, 49
Organizational chart, 33, 38